Mindreader

Mindreader

Find Out What People Really Think,
What They Really Want, AND
Who They Really Are

David J. Lieberman, PhD

RODALE.

New York

Published in the United States by Rodale Books, an imprint of Random House,
a division of Penguin Random House LLC, New York.
rodalebooks.com

RODALE and the Plant colophon are registered trademarks of
Penguin Random House LLC.

Library of Congress Cataloging-in-Publication Data
Names: Lieberman, David J., author.
Title: Mindreader : find out what people really think, what they really want,
and who they really are / David J. Lieberman, PhD.
Description: First edition. | New York : Rodale, [2022] | Includes
bibliographical references.
Identifiers: LCCN 2021047599 (print) | LCCN 2021047600 (ebook) |
ISBN 9780593236185 (hardcover) | ISBN 9780593236192 (ebook)
Subjects: LCSH: Psycholinguistics. | Body language. | Deception. |
Interpersonal communication—Psychological aspects.
Classification: LCC BF455 .L488 2022 (print) | LCC BF455 (ebook) |
DDC 401/.9—dc23/eng/20211216

ISBN 978-0-593-23618-5

Ebook ISBN 978-0-593-23619-2

Printed in the United States of America

Book design by Andrea Lau
Jacket design by Pete Garceau

10 9 8 7 6 5 4 3 2 1

First Edition

CONTENTS

PART II
49

The Human Lie Detector

PART III
91

Taking a Psychological Snapshot

CHAPTER 12 Activating the Defense Grid 113

When we take notice of how people see themselves and their world—what attracts their attention and what they avoid; what they mention and what they miss; what they accept and what they reject—we know their strengths, insecurities, and struggles.

CHAPTER 13 The Meaning of Values 121

The values that we hold announce to the world what matters to us most and paint a picture of our deepest selves. Pierce anyone's public persona and you'll know what makes them tick.

CHAPTER 14 The Resilience Factor 126

When a person is under pressure or dealing with stress, learn how to tell who will bend and who will break—and how to spot cracks before they even appear.

PART IV
Building a Psychological Profile

133

CHAPTER 15 In Search of Sanity 135

People who suffer from emotional illness share common language patterns, which broadcast their perceptions of reality. Learn all about a person's inner world in a single conversation.

CHAPTER 16 The Psychology of Self-Esteem 146

Uncover the myth of the self-loving narcissist and find out how to tell who has self-esteem and who suffers from a deep-seated feeling of inferiority and self-hatred.

CHAPTER 17 Unmasking Personality Disorders 153

Discover why some people push your buttons and your boundaries—and why you too often let them. More importantly, know how to spot any personality disorder type, including the well-hidden and polished sociopath.

Mindreader

Introduction

For thirty years, I've been developing psychological insights into human nature with strategies to enhance the quality of people's lives and relationships. In 1998, I wrote a book, called *Never Be Lied to Again,* that introduced specifically formulated techniques to help people detect deception in their everyday lives. Nearly a decade later, I wrote *You Can Read Anyone,* which was a follow-up to the first book and updated the science of reading people. Now, roughly another decade later, thanks to emerging research in psycholinguistics, neuroscience, and the cognitive and behavioral sciences, this new book takes a quantum leap forward. I will introduce you to the most advanced, cutting-edge methods in profiling people, which will give you near-telepathic abilities. In any situation—from a casual conversation to an in-depth negotiation—you will find what people really think and feel, regardless of what they claim. You will be privy to what lies deep in their subconscious mind, even when they themselves may be in denial and unwilling (or unable) to confront their thoughts, feelings, and fears on a conscious level.

Mindreader covers brand-new ground and relies little on age-old, outdated body language signs and signals. Many experts, for example, claim that crossed arms and legs suggest defensiveness or disagreement.

While this interpretation is not technically wrong, you will get a lot of false positives if your subject is seated in a cold room in a chair without an armrest. And yes, little or no direct eye contact is a classic sign of deception. But the bad guys already know this, so unless your subject is a five-year-old caught with his hand in an actual cookie jar, you'll need more sophisticated tactics. More chillingly, how do you accurately read a psychotic person who believes his own lies? Or a sociopath who looks you straight in the eyes and swears up and down on a stack of Bibles that he's telling the truth?[1]

We can now also move well beyond stereotypical strategies for reading people that purport to reveal stunning insights into the psyche based on superficial observations of dress. Does a religious pendant reflect deeply held spiritual values? Not necessarily. Maybe the person is wearing one to offset guilt because she lives antithetically to such ideals. Maybe she wears it for sentimental reasons, perhaps because it was her grandmother's. Do a power suit and well-shined shoes indicate ambition, and are sweatpants a sign of laziness? Not at all. Perhaps someone dresses casually because she's comfortable in her own skin and doesn't care what others think; then again, maybe she's grossly insecure but wants to appear not to care.

Another stalwart favorite is to extrapolate assumptions based on a single behavior. But this is nonsense. Just because your friend is always late doesn't necessarily mean he's inconsiderate. Maybe he's a perfectionist who has to have everything just right before he leaves. Maybe he gets an adrenaline rush by waiting until the last minute. Maybe his mother always insisted that he be on time and is leading a subconscious rebellion. Maybe he's a bit spacey and loses track of time. If we rely on surface assumptions, the opportunities to misread people are endless.

So what *does* work? The techniques I'll teach you herein draw from multiple disciplines—I teach these methods to the FBI's elite Behavioral Analysis Unit, the CIA, the NSA, almost every branch of the U.S. military, and law enforcement agencies around the world. All you have to do is pay attention to a few key elements, which will unveil a near-magical magnifying glass into a person's state of mind, his thoughts and feelings, and, most valuably, the degree of his integrity and emotional health.

Best of all, many of the techniques work without the need for interacting with your subject—oftentimes merely from listening to a conversation, speech, or recording, such as a voice-mail message. Or even from reading an email. The ability to read people, without having to see them, is ever more vital in an age when face masks and video conferencing can render even reliable facial and body language signs completely inert.

In the chapters to come, I'll show you step-by-step how to tell exactly what someone is thinking in real-life situations. For example, you will see precisely how to determine whether a person is trustworthy or dishonest, whether a coworker is troubled or just plain moody, or whether a first date is going your way or going south. And when the stakes are high—negotiations; interrogations; questions of abuse, theft, or fraud—you'll learn how to save yourself time, money, energy, and heartache by identifying who has your best interests at heart and who does not.

The reason my work is so widely used by law enforcement is because the techniques are easy to use and uncannily accurate, but only when used responsibly. I urge you not to abandon reason and common sense—or, for that matter, a relationship—due to a two-second surface read. It would be reckless to base your assumptions of a person's honesty, integrity, or intentions—let alone their emotional health—on an offhand remark or fleeting interaction.

Throughout this book single-sentence examples are used to illustrate the psychology. In real life, it would be prudent to rely on longer speech or writing samples before making any determination. As we will see throughout the book, a single, casual reference may not mean anything, but a consistent pattern of syntax reveals everything.[2]

When there's a lot on the line, take the time to build a reliable profile. Although this book is categorized into multiple parts and chapters, the methods I aim to teach you in each chapter are designed to build on the previous ones and should be folded into the process to enhance your overall assessment.

As you learn more about others, my hope is that you will also come to learn more about yourself and that with greater self-awareness you will gain the opportunity to enhance your own emotional health, life, and relationships. Enjoy a predictive edge in every conversation and situation—and in life itself—when you gain the ability to know what anyone is really thinking, what they really want, and who they really are.

Poker Corner

The game of poker is, in many ways, a psychological lab of human behavior and serves as a wonderful real-life metaphor in which tactics can be employed to read people. Even if you're unacquainted with the game, I think you will enjoy these insights and applications as we move through the book.

PART I

SUBCONSCIOUS REVEALS

From a casual conversation to an in-depth negotiation, find out what people really think and feel. You will be privy to what lies deep in their subconscious mind—even when they themselves may be in denial and unwilling or unable to confront their thoughts, feelings, and fears on a conscious level. Discover what people really think about you and how much power and control they believe they have in all of their relationships, both personal and professional.

CHAPTER 1

What They *Really* Think

By paying close attention not only to what people say but also to *how* they say it—their language pattern and sentence structure—you can figure out what's really going on inside their head. To demonstrate how this works, we begin with a quick and painless grammar lesson.

A personal pronoun, in the grammatical sense, is associated with a certain individual or group of individuals. It can be subjective, objective, or possessive, depending on usage. Grammatically speaking, when discussing a person or persons, there are three separate perspectives:

- First person (i.e., *I, me, my,* and *mine* or *we, us, our,* and *ours*)
- Second person (i.e., *you, your,* and *yours*)
- Third person (i.e., *he, him,* and *his; she, her,* and *hers;* and *they, them,* and *theirs*)

On the surface, it might seem as if pronouns simply replace nouns so that people don't have to repeat the same words over and over again. "John lost John's wallet somewhere in John's house" is not exactly an elegant sentence. "John lost his wallet somewhere in his house" just sounds better. But from a psycholinguistic standpoint, pronouns can reveal whether someone is trying to distance or altogether separate himself from his words. In much the same way that an unsophisticated liar might look away from you because eye contact increases intimacy and a person who is lying often feels a degree of guilt, a person making an untrue statement often seeks to subconsciously distance himself from his own words. The personal pronouns (e.g., *I, me, mine,* and *my*) indicate that a person is committed to and confident about his statement. Omitting personal pronouns from the action may signal someone's reluctance to accept ownership of his words.

Let's take the everyday example of giving a compliment. A woman who believes what she's saying is more likely to use a personal pronoun—for instance, "I really liked your presentation," or "I loved what you said in the meeting." However, a person offering insincere flattery might choose to say "Nice presentation" or "Looks like you did a lot of research." In the second case, she has removed herself from the equation entirely. Those in law enforcement are well acquainted with this principle and recognize when people are filing a false report about their car being stolen because they typically refer to it as "the car" or "that car" and not "my car" or "our car." Of course, you can't gauge a person's honesty by a single sentence, but it's the first clue.

A Distant Second

Even when a personal pronoun is present, a switch from *active* to *passive voice* may signify a lack of sincerity. The active voice is stronger and more directly interactive, revealing that the subject—the person or the people, in our examples—performs the action of the verb in the sentence. With the passive voice, the subject is acted upon by some other entity.

For example, "I gave her the pen" is in active voice, while "The pen was given to her by me" uses passive voice. Notice the shift in phrasing and how it subtly decreases the speaker's personal responsibility. To wit, let's say that two siblings are playing, and the younger one starts to cry. Most of the time, when mom or dad asks what's going on, the reason the child is crying—as stated by the other child—is because "he fell," "she got hurt," or "he banged his head." A child rarely says, "I did (action A) that caused (consequence B)." Indeed, it's unusual for a child (the egocentric beings that they are) to assume responsibility and declare: "I pushed him into the wall, and he hit his head," or "I should have been more careful when she climbed on my back."

Let's look at this in another context. In a study titled "Words That Cost You the Job Interview," researchers assessed the interview language of hundreds of thousands of real-life job candidates. Based on language patterns alone, they successfully divided these candidates into low and high performers.[1] Here's what they found:

- High-performer answers contain roughly 60 percent more first-person pronouns (e.g., *I, me, we*).
- Low-performer answers contain about 400 percent more second-person pronouns (e.g., *you, your*).
- Low-performer answers contain about 90 percent more third-person pronouns (e.g., *he, she, they*).

High performers put themselves front and center in the action because they can call upon actual experiences. Low performers don't. They can't. They are more likely to give abstract or hypothetical answers because they lack real-world experience and success.[2]

High-performer language: "I call my customers every month to see how they're doing." Or "I made two hundred calls every day at ABC Corp."

Low-performer language: "Customers should be contacted regularly." Or "You [or one] should always call the customer and ask them to share . . ."

When you take yourself out of the proverbial action, you send a concealed message (possibly even from yourself). Ask a child about her first day at camp, and note how the same summation reveals two different impressions of her experience: the first, more enthusiastic and the second, lackluster:

> **RESPONSE A**: "I ate breakfast, then we went over to the park to play on the swings until I got to go swimming."
>
> **RESPONSE B**: "First, it was breakfast, then they moved us over to the park to play on the swings until they sent us to the swimming pool."

The use of the passive tense or the absence of a pronoun also softens a message that may be ill received or confrontational. For example, one might excitedly proclaim, "We won the game!" but not "The game was won [by us]" because the active voice with a personal pronoun conveys solidarity with the message, thus invoking an assumption of pleasure and pride. Likewise, politicians tend to phrase reluctant admissions or apologies to dilute direct responsibility, including such gems as "Mistakes were made," "The truth had some deficits," and "The people deserve better." The phraseology also hints to the character of the speaker. When your tailor informs you that "I made a mistake on your hem," rather than, "A mistake was made," we can surmise that he operates with a greater degree of honesty and integrity.[3]

The Great Divide

Distancing language assumes many shapes and sizes. Take a look at the following pairs of phrases and ask yourself which ones strike the chord of greater authenticity.

"I stand in awe" versus "I'm in awe."

"I find myself filled with pride" versus "I am so proud."

"I, for one, am glad" versus "I'm so glad."

"I am a great admirer" versus "I greatly admire."

The first phrasings are all attempts to imprint the message with an emotional intensity but fail in convincing the keen observer because of two linguistic giveaways. First, a heightened emotional state is associated with a simplified grammatical structure, not the more florid ones. Sincere, emotionally laden sentences are short and to the point. Think: "Help!" or "I love you." Second, the speaker creates a separation between himself (the "I") and the emotional sentiment. Which of these statements sounds more believable?

STATEMENT A: "I'm so grateful that my wife was found alive. I'm indebted to all of the rescue workers."

STATEMENT B: "I, for one, am so grateful that my wife was found alive. I find myself indebted to all of the rescue workers."

Statement A resonates as heartfelt while Statement B feels like a PR release. The second statement is not worrisome if the speaker has had time to compose himself and his thoughts. However, an impromptu, emotionally charged situation should exhibit a language pattern more consistent with Statement A.

At such times, clichés and metaphors are also highly suspect. A person using them in an attempt to portray himself as impassioned is trying to economically convey an emotion that is not real. Manufacturing emotion takes lot of mental energy, so the person uses borrowed phrases. For example, ask any trauma victim about what happened, and you will not get a Nietzschean quote such as "To live is to suffer; to survive is to find some meaning in the suffering" or a cliché such as "That's the way the cookie crumbles."

Certainly, with the passage of time and a shift in perspective, we may adopt a more philosophical view. Yet no one will ever convey an emotionally charged encounter by reciting the latest Pinterest quote on the beauty of suffering. Likewise, if someone proffers that a traumatic experience is "indelibly in my amygdala" (emotional memories are stored in this part of the brain), it reeks of inauthenticity. There needs to be emotional congruence.

Far-reaching research into real-life, high-stakes public appeals for help with missing relatives found that genuine pleas contained more verbal expressions of hope of finding the missing person alive, more positive emotions toward the relative, and an avoidance of brutal or harsh language.[4] In short, the pleas are rich with raw emotion and optimism rather than mottos and slogans peppered with negativity.

Euphemistically Speaking

Faux silk is polyester. Leatherette is made from plastic. Manufacturers do not label their goods to deceive per se but rather to alter perceptions. After all, some words strike a negative visceral chord. Euphemisms can help blunt the emotional impact. It is for this reason that good salespeople won't tell you to "sign the contract" but will rather suggest that you "okay the paperwork." Even though both phrases point to the same action, it has been ingrained in us that we should be wary of signing a contract without first having a lawyer review it. But okaying paperwork, that's something you can do without worrying, right?

A skilled interrogator knows to avoid harsh words or phrases—such as *embezzlement, murder, lying, confession*—and to stay away from language that pits him against his subject. For instance, rather than insisting, "Stop lying and tell me the truth," they'd say, "Let's hear the whole story" or "Let's clear the air for everyone's sake."

Politicians understand more than most people the power of words to influence attitudes and behavior. During a military action, we would rather hear of "collateral damage" than be told that civilians were accidentally killed, and we are not as disturbed hearing of "friendly fire" as we would be to learn that our soldiers shot at one another. And, of course, when watching the morning news, we are less moved being told of "casualties" than we would be if the reporter used the word *deaths*.

In everyday life, we do the same thing: We may refer to the toilet as the bathroom, powder room, men's room, or ladies' room. Indeed, we would rather tell our insurance company of the "fender bender" than use the word *collision*. And, of course, letting an employee "go" or telling him he is being "laid off" is often the preferred language over being "fired."

The use of a euphemism informs us that the individual wants to dilute or deflect directness and may be (a) attempting to minimize their request or their deeds, (b) concerned that their message will be ill received, (c) uncomfortable with the topic itself, or (d) any combination thereof.

Here and *There*

A person's subconscious effort to associate himself—with his listener, the content of his communication, or the object of communication—is also achieved through the use of what's called *spatial immediacy*.[5] Adverbs like *this* and *that, these* and *those,* and *here* and *there* show where a person or an object is in relation to the speaker. These words also illuminate emotional distance. Oftentimes we use spatial immediacy to refer to someone or something that we feel positive toward and want to be associated with (e.g., "*This* is an interesting idea" or "*Here* is an interesting idea"). It is important to note that the converse is not instructive. A colleague who says, "*That's* an interesting idea," is not necessarily feigning enthusiasm. Language that reflects closeness and connection is correlated with one's feelings, but a parallel should not be assumed with distancing language.

The psychological intricacies abound because distancing language may indicate a psychological defense mechanism called *detachment*. In a therapeutic setting, for example, an astute analyst is aware that when a patient frequently avoids or omits personal pronouns, they may be trying to avoid intimacy, candor, or responsibility.[6] Be alert to the use of a second-person pronoun such as *you* or the third-person *one*. Although these are often meant in a universal context that applies to everyone ("You should always say *please* and *thank you*"), the use of *you* or *one* when we mean *I* or *my* does signal emotional unease. For example, imagine that a manager tells an employee to better manage his workflow and not wait until the last minute to take care of important issues. Consider two possible responses:

> **RESPONSE A:** "I know, but I just can't always predict what will come up."
>
> **RESPONSE B:** "You know, you just can't always predict what will come up."

Although neither response embraces the rebuke, the second one deflects it altogether because the employee is declaring that predicting what might come up is a universal problem rather than acknowledging his own weakness with time management. In chapter 12, you will learn how to identify when a conversation hits a raw emotional nerve and to differentiate between the person who is lying to you from one who is lying to himself.

Poker Corner

A number of fascinating research studies have found that people subconsciously associate their dominant side—as in being right- or left-handed—with positivity and optimism and associate their nondominant side with more negative ideas and constructs. It appears that the linking of *good* with *dominant* extends to most areas of our lives.[7] (To determine the dominant hand, take note of how people reach for objects they are handed—or, better, those thrown directly in front of them so neither hand is closer.) In my own research, I have found that a player who is bluffing will put the chips into the pot using his nondominant hand a substantial majority of the time. Although this is not a hard-and-fast rule, it is a reliable indicator in conjunction with other signs.

This chapter has introduced only the linguistic groundwork. Much more goes into the grammatical soup, so I'll just offer the reminder again that it would be ludicrous to suggest that a single sentence is hard proof of anything. Consider, for example, that extroverts tend to bring their linguistic selves into their preferences (e.g., "I found it interesting"), while an introvert's evaluation may be from arm's length ("It's interesting"). As an isolated statement, neither declaration can be said to be more or less believable. We also learned that the active voice lends credence but may be offset with the lack of a personal pronoun. For example, the sentence "The book is fascinating," uses an active voice, while "I was fascinated by the book" contains "I" ownership with a passive voice. Differentiating between deception and detachment is likewise difficult when based on a solitary remark.

As you progress through this book, the psychology will become more intricate and our tactics more sophisticated. We're just getting started!

CHAPTER 2

How a Person Sees and Feels about Other People

Those in law enforcement know that victims of violent crimes, such as abduction or assault, rarely use the word *we*. Instead, they'll relate the events in a way that separates them from the aggressor, referring to the attacker as "he" or "she" and themselves as "I." Rather than say, for example, "We got into the car," they are inclined to phrase it as "He put me in the car"; and rather than say "We stopped for gas," they might word it as "He stopped for gas." Recounting a story that is peppered with *we, us,* and *our* may indicate psychological closeness (certainly not expected in a crime) and implies an association, a relationship, and perhaps even cooperation.[1]

We can observe benign applications of this in everyday life. At the end of a date, Jack and Jill walk out of a restaurant, and Jill inquires, "Where did we park the car?" An innocent question, but using *we* instead of *you* indicates that she has begun to identify with Jack and sees them as a couple. Asking "Where is *your* car parked?" hardly implies disinterest, if, in fact, it is Jack's car; but turning *your* into *our* does expose a subtext of interest.

Whenever I speak to couples, I'm always on the lookout when the word *we* is conspicuously absent from any conversation. Research finds that married couples who use cooperative language (e.g., *we, our,* and *us*), more often than individualized language (e.g., *I, me,* and *you*) have lower divorce rates and report greater marital satisfaction.[2] Studies also demonstrate a powerful correlation between such pronoun use and how couples respond to disagreements and crises, predicting whether they will team up and cooperate or become polarized and divided.[3] The use of *you*-words (e.g., *you, your,* and *yourself*) may suggest unexpressed frustration or outright aggression. In conversation, a person who says, "You need to figure this out," conveys enmity and a "me versus you" mindset. However, "We need to figure this out" indicates "us versus the problem," a presumption of shared responsibility and cooperation.

Can you guess whose marriage is in more dire straits?

PERSON A: "Our marriage is in trouble."
PERSON B: "The marriage is in trouble."

Person B doesn't simply distance himself from his spouse but detaches altogether from the marriage. It exists as some entity outside of himself. Other examples abound: Speaking about "my children" versus "our children" when in the presence of one's spouse or about shared spaces as "my house" or "my bedroom" informs us of the person's perspective. Likewise, an agitated parent may well ask her spouse, "Do you know what your son did in class?" in reference to something undesirable, while a positive situation may sound more like "Do you know what my [or our] son did in class?" Again, a single, casual reference does not mean anything (and any of these statements might signal someone's anger or frustration *in the moment*, not about the marriage itself), but a consistent pattern of syntax reveals everything.

The implications and applications of syntax extend to the corporate arena as well. Research finds that firms where workers typically refer to their workplace as "the company" or "that company" rather than "my company" or "our company," and to coworkers mostly as "they" rather

A single, casual reference does not mean anything, but a consistent pattern of syntax reveals everything.

than "my coworkers," are likely to have low morale and a high rate of turnover.[4] Same goes in sports, where a fair-weather fan can be spotted through his language: When the fan's team wins, they characteristically declare, "We won." But when the team loses, it becomes "They lost," because, again, the pronoun *we* is typically reserved for positive associations and affiliations.

The King and I

When a person offers up information, its sequence is significant. If someone brings up people, objects, or even emotions in what seems to be a random order that is not integral or logical to the flow of a conversation, we would do well to pay attention to that order. It typically broadcasts the person's subconscious priorities or indicates that he or she would rather not discuss certain things.

You can remember this ancient but revealing insight into human nature, courtesy of a biblical story. Two women came before the wisest of men, King Solomon. They had each given birth to a baby boy a few days apart. While sleeping, one of the women accidentally rolled onto her baby, suffocating him. She then switched her baby with the living one, but when the mother of that child woke up, she realized it wasn't her son and knew the babies had been switched.

Solomon already knew through prophecy who the living child's mother was, but he wanted to demonstrate his thinking with irrefutable logic. He exclaimed, "This one says, 'My son is the live one, and the dead one is your son,' and this one says, 'Not so, your son is the dead one, and my son is the live one.'"

Then Solomon asked for his sword and explained he would resolve the situation by dividing the living baby in half. One woman screamed, "No!" This, of course, indicated she was the mother of the living child. The legendary lie detection expert Avinoam Sapir aptly points out that the second woman told the king, "Her son is dead. Mine is alive," but the first mentioned her own child first ("My son is alive. Hers is dead.") because her focus was on her own child—who was alive—and she accordingly prioritized him in her exclamation.[5] Sapir cites another example from a "Dear Abby" letter:

> A woman wrote that her son had some sort of a problem, but her husband was not understanding. She wanted to know what she could do to make her husband understand. But in the letter, the woman mentioned herself, her son, and her son's dog before she mentioned her husband. And she gave the names of her son and the dog but didn't name her husband. "She rates the dog ahead of her husband," showing that her real problem is with her husband, not the husband's relationship with the son.[6]

This general rule of noting the order of details applies across a wide spectrum of situations and scenarios. For instance, when you ask a child about the members of her family, she may respond, "My mother, my father," and then rattle off the names of a few siblings. Certainly, we shouldn't assume something is wrong if she says "Daddy" before "Mommy," lists the siblings in birth order, or mentions her two sisters and then her "annoying" baby brother. Moreover, if Spotty, the dog, and Goldie, the goldfish, are mentioned before mom or dad, there's no reason for concern, particularly when it comes to small children. However, if a family member is absent or at the end of the list, after stuffed animals, pets, and the like, then further inquiry may be warranted. To be clear, the order or absence of a family member does not indicate that something nefarious is afoot, but it does tell us that their relationship is different from what we may have assumed.

Similarly, when you ask an employee about her work environment, she might talk about "my supervisor" and then bring up some of her colleagues. We shouldn't assume that anything is amiss if she merely puts one associate before another, lists colleagues in hierarchical order, or first mentions her sister-in-law, the receptionist.[7] However, if she starts talking about the coffee machine and the break room before colleagues or friends, this might suggest feelings of social isolation, aloofness, or lack of affinity for others in the workplace and be worthy of deeper investigation.

I recently met a childhood friend whom I had not seen in about thirty years. After the obligatory exchange of lies, "Wow, you look great . . . you haven't changed a bit," it was picture time. He proceeded to show me a number of photos of him and his dog eating lunch in the park, snuggling in bed, and catching a Frisbee at the beach. Then he caught me up on the celebrities he was "tight with," his finger swiping through selfies with his B-list chums. Dozens of photos and an eternity later, he stopped on a photo of a teenage boy: dumbbells in hand, shirtless, and solo. "That's my son, Mark," he said plainly. A single swipe revealed the next photo. "That's my daughter." He gave no name. "She's at UCLA." End of commentary. Neither of his children's photos featured dad. My old friend was still married to wife number two, but there was no mention of her. No photo of her. Nothing about her.

Does it mean he doesn't love his wife and children? No. Maybe he desperately wants to connect with his family, but any number of personal issues or unknown circumstances might make it difficult. In that case, their relationship is strained, and his affection goes to his dog. Or, perhaps, he is egotistical, entirely self-consumed, and has zero interest in his family. He builds up a faltering self-image by showing off his celebrity acquaintances. We don't know for sure, based on this brief exchange, but we do know with certainty that his relationship with his wife and children is not rosy, and this is something that he never intended to disclose to me.

All of the above holds true in impromptu conversations and situations where forethought is not assumed. In guarded instances—such as a negotiation or mediation—a seasoned professional is unlikely to initially express his real interest to avoid losing leverage. The very fact, then, that a person completely ignores something that would presumably attract his attention (the five-hundred-pound gorilla) tells us that this may be something that *does* interest him.

Many years ago, I invited an art dealer to my home to look at five paintings that were left to me after my great-aunt had died. I hadn't done my due diligence, as this guy was a "friend of a friend of a friend." After glancing at the collection for a few silent minutes, he made a call and then said something to the effect of, "There's really not much here. Maybe this one [pointing to one picture] is worth a few hundred bucks, but I can put them all in the clearance section of my gallery and get a few thousand dollars. How about I give you three thousand dollars for everything?" Now, I don't know much about art. Okay, nothing. But I do know about human nature, and I noticed that he had completely ignored one small painting. I found this curious because he gave all of the other ones at least a two-second glance, even those that he subsequently declared "worthless."

I declined his offer and thanked him for his time. His offer went up. I declined. It went up again. After a few more rounds and several "final" offers, it became abundantly clear that he could not be trusted. He left none too pleased, and I phoned an art appraiser (not a dealer, but one who charges a fee for his services). It turned out that while four of the five paintings—including the one that the art dealer said was worth something—weren't worth the canvas they were painted on, the one small painting he had ignored was worth approximately seven times his "final" offer.

Symbolic Representation

A new mother is folding her infant's laundry. As she picks each tiny, lovingly purchased item out of the basket and smooths it out, she smiles. She stacks the fresh laundry neatly and places it in the drawer of the baby's bureau. With a small sigh of satisfaction, she admires her handiwork and shuts the drawer.

Through her blissful execution of this otherwise tedious chore, the mother reveals the contents of her heart; she treasures her baby. We know this is so because she handles the baby's belongings with such love and care. Similarly, a person may cherish an item that belonged to beloved parents or grandparents; the item itself might be better suited for the recycling bin, but this person treats it like a precious heirloom. The concept of symbolic representation, illustrated by these scenarios, states that we can discern how someone feels about another person by observing how they treat objects associated with that person. In math, this is the transitive property: If $A = B$ and $B = C$, then $A = C$. Of course, in psychology, unlike mathematics, this is not a hard-and-fast rule. But it *is* another window through which we can gain understanding of others' behaviors.

Symbolic representation can reveal important insights that may be difficult to glean in a more straightforward way. For example, a patient who had abruptly divorced her second husband (after a three-month marriage) was concerned about her young daughter's adjustment to her stepfather's absence. I suggested that she give her daughter a teddy bear and tell her that it was from her stepfather. If the child hugged the teddy bear and held it close, the mother could assume that she missed her stepfather. If, on the other hand, she seemed disinterested in it, she could infer that the child felt little, if any, emotional attachment to him. If she was distraught—and angry with him—she may exhibit destructive behavior toward the bear and throw it aside callously or try to pull its little glued-on eyes off its furry head. Once again, I didn't suggest we should draw a conclusive interpretation, but the way she treated the representative (of her stepfather) teddy bear would point us in the right direction.

We all navigate the emotional space between ourselves and others through a variety of linguistic mechanisms. Simply by listening for slight shifts in language we can gauge whether someone wants to be closer or is looking to create distance between us or themselves and another. This is useful when we want to figure out the level of rapport in any relationship, old or new. In the next chapter we'll build on our skill set with methods that quickly determine who is enthusiastic and who is apathetic, in any conversation and context.

CHAPTER 3

Close Encounters

We're all familiar with the idea of finishing someone else's sentences. With a shared outlook, we see things the same way; each person is tuned in to the other. At the opposite end of the spectrum, interrupting another person to inject a "different ending," based on your own perspective, indicates friction. The phrase *Let me finish* is baked into many such conversations. Put simply, when the ego is engaged, we don't want to let other people into our physical or emotional space, and we certainly don't want to be interrupted.

In *The Secret Life of Pronouns*, social psychologist and linguistic pioneer, James W. Pennebaker unearths a network of correlations between language, thought, and personality. He explains that the use of what are called *function words*—even by those whom we have just met—reflects and fortifies an emotional bridge and indicates their desire to let us into their space and to enhance our emotional synchronicity.[1] Research finds that an increase in function words positively predicts mutually successful outcomes in almost every arena, from the cohesiveness of a work group to the peaceful resolution of a hostage negotiation.[2]

To best explain how this works, it's time for another quick grammar lesson.

There are two classes of speech: content words and function words. Content words are nouns, verbs, adjectives, and most adverbs (e.g., *cash, breathe, learn, tall, slowly*).[3] They communicate the gist of the message—the substance and the main content of what is being said. Function words, such as pronouns, prepositions, and articles, are the grammatical glue that provides cohesion and fluency (e.g., *I, over, at, through, in, an, the*). These words have little or no meaning outside the context of the sentence and require shared knowledge or the same frame of reference to be understood.[4] For example, to comprehend the sentence "He put them over there" requires both the speaker and the listener to have a common perspective. Both parties know who "he" is, what "them" refers to, and where "there" is.

For this reason, an angry person—one who is uninterested in a shared experience, much less a connection—employs concrete, unambiguous language because it is *you* versus *him*. There is no *us* or *we*. This means the use of unequivocal syntax with a complete subject and pronoun (e.g., "I told you not to let the dog out of the backyard" rather than "I told you not to let him out of there"). The meaning of the first sentence is explicit and does not rely on a mutual point of reference.

When you were young and your mother called you by your full name, you knew that you were in trouble. Likewise, with our spouse, when we're in hot water, terms of endearment are few and far between. But if they're calling us "sweetheart" or "lovey" (please see *Gilligan's Island* reruns for this dated reference), then we're probably not in too much trouble. Consider the following pair of sentences:

- **STATEMENT 1:** "Remember, I asked you to put them over there when you got back from seeing her."
- **STATEMENT 2:** "Remember, I asked you to put the keys in the kitchen next to the toaster the minute you came back from your sister's house."

Note that the first sentence, which is rich with function words, is less intense than the second sentence, which has more content words. Spoken softly, the tone of the first sentence shifts and may be heard like a gentle reminder. Do the same with the second sentence, and the anger still comes through with a quiet intensity, much like someone seething and trying hard to keep from exploding.[5]

Let's take another example, where you find yourself at an office party and an all-too-intoxicated colleague comes over to rub your shoulders. An unbridled angry reaction would be clear and definitive (e.g., "Take your hands off me"; "I don't want you touching me"; "Who asked you to come over here and touch me?"). The speaker leaves no room for misunderstanding.[6] A more submissive response—which reflects the person's personality or lower status—is conveyed through linguistic softening that minimizes or eliminates the content words (e.g., "I don't really like that"; "Oh, no, thanks").

New Encounters

When two people meet, the more quickly they establish a shared perspective, the more they seek to share the experience and forge a connection.[7] An increase in function words shows not only each person's attempts to engage the other but also the degree to which these efforts are reciprocated.[8] Let's take two looks at a generic scenario with near-identical interactions, except the first exchange uses more function words; the second, more content words.

Scene 1, Take 1

Waiting in Line at a Coffee Shop, Boy Meets Girl

Boy: Wow, sure is crowded.
Girl: Yeah, it's always like this here.

Boy: Really? Crazy long line.

Girl: Yup, but it really moves.

Boy: Fast?

Girl: Super.

Boy: That's good because it's boiling in here.

Girl: Yeah, I know.

Boy: Do you work nearby?

Girl: Yeah, over at Onyx on—

Boy: Oh, on Bleecker? The big black building?

Girl: That's the one. You?

Boy: I'm over at Carlson's Tavern.

Girl: The new one?

Boy: Yup, all shiny and—

Girl: Bright with red paint.

Boy: That's the one . . . I'm up next.

Girl: Oh . . . Enjoy.

This sounds like a typical, mildly flirty exchange between two young people enjoying pleasant chitchat while in line. Now let's change the language slightly and you'll see how quickly our perception of their interaction shifts.

Scene 1, Take 2

Waiting in Line at a Coffee Shop, Boy Meets Girl

Boy: Wow, sure is crowded.

Girl: Yes, Coffee Queen is always crowded.

Boy: Really? Crazy long line.

Girl: It is a long line, but it moves fast.

Boy: That's good because it's boiling in here.

Girl: It is warm in here.

Boy: Do you work nearby?

```
Girl:  Yup.
Boy:   Where abouts?
Girl:  I work over at Onyx.
Boy:   Do you like working there?
Girl:  I do.
Boy:   I work over at Carlson's Tavern.
Girl:  Oh, okay.
Boy:   Yup, they repainted it bright red.
Girl:  Ahh.
Boy:   I'm up next.
Girl:  Okay, enjoy your coffee.
```

The girl is now polite but is obviously less interested here.

Let's continue to play out the scene whereby the barista hands the girl both drinks, and she, in turn, gives the boy's drink to him. Take note of each phrasing:

- "There's your drink."
- "Here we are."

These three simple words can reveal a treasure trove of information.

- "There's [nonimmediate, signaling distance] your [oppositional] drink [concrete noun]."
- "Here [immediate, signaling closeness] we [united, a bond] are [function word, relying on shared knowledge]."

When a teacher hands back a marked test, a chef presents a new dish, or an architect unrolls a set of blueprints, there is a world of difference between "Here we are" and "There you go."

The logic is crystallized when we think of someone who is terribly upset with another person. It is unlikely that he would say, "Here we are," unless he's offering up a poisoned drink. Although I can't overstate the danger of reading too much into a single phrase—and "There you go" does not signal hidden disdain—language that reflects closeness and connection is a reliable indication that one person

When a teacher hands back a marked test, a chef presents a new dish, or an architect unrolls a set of blueprints, there is a world of difference between "Here we are" and "There you go."

is, at the very least, not hopping mad at the other. In other words, it's important to reemphasize that "There you go" should not be construed as emotional distance but that "Here we are" can be read as emotional closeness.

Can I Have Your Attention, Please!

What do words and phrases like these have in common?

believe it or not
actually
as a matter of fact
basically
as it turns out
honestly
essentially

I call these *conversational spotlights*. They are used to draw attention to what we are saying when we want to magnify the significance of our message. Remarkably, they indicate two entirely different things based on the context of the interaction. When used by someone who is trying to sway another—a guilty suspect being interrogated—their use may indicate deception (see chapter 6). However, when used (nonsarcastically) in a casual conversation they mean that the person is open and interested in the conversation and is trying to engage and perhaps impress. Let's pepper our coffee shop exchange with a few of these conversational spotlights. Note how they suggest a budding connection.

Scene 1, Take 3

Waiting in Line at a Coffee Shop, Boy Meets Girl

Boy: Wow, sure is crowded.

Girl: Yeah, believe it or not, it's always like this here.

Boy: Really? Crazy long line.

Girl: Yup, but it really moves.

Boy: Fast?

Girl: Super.

Boy: That's good because it's boiling in here.

Girl: Yeah, I know.

Boy: Do you work nearby?

Girl: Yeah, as a matter of fact, I'm over at Onyx on—

Boy: Oh, on Bleecker? The big black building?

Girl: That's the one. You?

Boy: Actually, I'm over at Carlson's Tavern.

Girl: The new one?

Boy: Yup, all shiny and—

Girl: Bright with red paint.

Boy: You know it; that's the one . . . I'm up next.

Girl: Oh, okay . . . Enjoy.

Recall that even in uncomfortable circumstances—à la our intoxicated colleague scenario on page 22—some people have difficulty asserting themselves and expressing their disinterest. To do so would simply be "impolite." The language patterns that people use in relationships—both personal and professional—also expose their perception of status and control within the relationship, even one that's five minutes old. More profoundly, how people see others and view relationships discloses a wealth of insight into their emotional health. In the next chapter, we will begin to decode the language of power and personality.

CHAPTER 4

Relationship Status and Power

An unwritten cross-cultural rule is that lower status people don't give commands to those of higher status; they thus soften their language when making a request. For example, a flight attendant will invite passengers to "take their seats" rather than to "sit down." Common sense and research align with a positive correlation between status and politeness.[1] When you ask a favor or make a request of someone, the language is calibrated to the size of the request and the power gap between the two people.[2] Lower status (or overall insecurity) is revealed through the degree to which a person feels it's necessary to modify her requests.[3] We do this through any one, or a combination, of ten mechanisms:

1. Just add *please*: "Pass the salt" becomes "Please pass the salt."
2. Turn the request into a question: "Close the door" becomes "Can you close the door?"
3. Use upspeak, meaning a rise in intonation at the end of the sentence: "Close the door" becomes "Close the door?"
4. Minimize or hedge the request: "Can you stay later?" becomes "Can you stay just a little bit later?" or "Perhaps you might stay a bit longer?"

5. Apologize for the request: "I need you to come in early" becomes "I'm sorry to do this, but . . ."
6. Ask the request indirectly: "What time is it?" becomes "Do you have the time?"
7. Frame the request as a rule: Rather than make a request, the person is apprised of the standing policy. "Stop diving in the pool" becomes "Diving is not allowed."
8. State the facts: "Take out the garbage" becomes "The garbage is full."
9. Present the possibility: "Put your credit card in now" becomes "You can put in your card now."
10. Ask if you can ask: Instead of making the request, start with "Can I ask you a favor . . ."

Asking if you can ask removes the threat entirely and is illustrated in the following story. A good friend of mine is the head fundraiser for a large nonprofit organization. Each day he asks people for hundreds of thousands, sometimes millions, of dollars. Occasionally, he will go back to the same donor—someone who just gave money a mere month ago—and ask for another donation. While some people think this is an unusual practice, he always develops great relationships with these donors. What is his secret to avoid offending them? Simple. He doesn't ask for another donation. Instead, he asks whether he can ask for a donation. Do you see the difference in the dynamics? If he were to ask for money outright, he would put the other person on the defensive and risk coming across as ungrateful, thus creating a power struggle. But by asking whether he can ask, he puts the donor in control and, as such, eliminates the donor's defenses. Why? Because the donor can simply say no to the question, without having to say no to the request for money.

> When you ask a favor or make a request of someone, the language is calibrated to the size of the request and the power gap between the two people.

If the absence of a linguistic softener signals higher status (actual or perceived), combining two or more softeners into a single request is equally illuminating of lower status or of a submissive personality. Take, for instance, a doubly solicitous request windup: "I'm so sorry to trouble you, but could I possibly ask if you might . . ." There's no missing the fact that the speaker is "managing up" here. One's acknowledgment can also assume many forms, ranging from an overly polite "Thank you so much" to ungrateful silence.

No discussion of the communication of status and power in conversation would be complete without mentioning the potential to misread the use of the "royal we." It may be indicative of a higher status individual who wants to avoid a tacit "me versus you" dynamic. The lady of the house who tells the cleaning help, "We need to wash the floors," has little intention of getting out the mop and pail herself. Likewise, the drill sergeant in basic training rebukes a trainee with "Drop and give me fifty," not "Let's drop. We need to do some push-ups here." However, a lower status person may also use this language to avoid a direct inquiry or request. A secretary, may, for instance, ask his boss, "Can we wrap up work by five o'clock?" rather than, "Can I leave at five o'clock?" or "Will you be done by five o'clock, so I can go home?"

Silence Is Golden

Another unwritten rule of power is that the less you have to say or do to gain cooperation, the more control you have. To wit, we would expect to observe a higher-ranking officer gesture to another officer or cadet to move, stop, sit down, and the like, without ever saying a word. Likewise, with a wave of the hand, the police stop traffic, and with a finger raised in the air, the judge silences the attorney. To exert influence over another—to move him or to stop him—is to exercise status, and the less pressure you need to apply to gain cooperation, the more power you wield and the more control you have.

Emotionally healthy lower status people are less likely to issue nonverbal commands to those of higher status. Could you imagine a new recruit in basic training holding up his hand to the drill sergeant as if to say, "Wait!"?

This rule is observable across multiple domains. Take classroom management, for example. A revered or even feared teacher holds up her hand as if to say, "Stop," and the class falls silent. She does not need to speak, much less plead. She is in charge. There is no power struggle. We would, of course, be shocked to witness a student gesturing for his teacher to stop talking or to sit down. A student verbally interrupting the teacher is, however, less jarring because the student's awareness of the status dynamic is not so corrupted as to believe that his teacher will heed a nonverbal command. Any parent will instantly relate to how this plays out with her own children. The less the parent has to say to correct her child's behavior, the greater her authority in the relationship. If a mother's stern look is all that is required for her child to take her feet off the couch, she has a different relationship with her child than the parent whose child ignores her look of disapproval, displays obvious annoyance, or erupts in back talk. A child's refusal to comply altogether with the parent's will—despite multiple, increasingly louder requests—makes it quite clear who is really in charge.

Accordingly, a person may become infuriated when someone of lower status gives him a nonverbal command, such as raising a pointer finger midair, as if to say, "Shush" or "Wait"; pointing a finger at him, as if to say, "Hey you"; or gesturing for him to slow down while driving, as if to say, "Listen to me." In fact, in any given interaction, the lower status person rarely points a finger at the other(s). Finger-pointing indicates conviction and authority, as well as confidence in our position. Observe any two people speaking, even when you can't hear what they are saying, and the one who is pointing is the one with the power (or who feels empowered because he believes he holds the higher moral ground).

Inward or Outward Focus

Here's the scene: You witness one person march into the office of another. She closes the door so you cannot make out her question. You do, however, overhear the response, which is either:

RESPONSE A: "What are you talking about?"
RESPONSE B: "I don't know what you're talking about."

If you were to guess, which response would indicate that person sitting in the office is of a higher status than the one who marched into it? Don't feel bad if you get it wrong. Most people do.

Response A indicates a person of higher status. It's counterintuitive, explains psychologist James Pennebaker, that people who have power tend to use *I, me,* and *my* fewer times than do those of lower status. This is because pronouns signal our focus.[4] We become self-oriented when we feel insecure and defensive, and we are outwardly oriented when we feel empowered and in control.[5]

Our perception of status leaks through subtleties in even the briefest exchanges and interactions. Consider the difference between "You should know" and "I would like you to know." "You should know" comes from a place of high status because it is (a) outwardly focused and (b) worded as a fact—that is, "You should know something." By contrast, the second phrase implies said information is not necessary for you to know, but it is something that "I" would like to share with you. The focus is on *my* needs, not *yours.* Let's take an example of two short text messages to see how so many indications can be packed into so few words.

RESPONSE A: "Good morning and forgive the delay in getting back to you. Agreed, it looks good. Nice job."
RESPONSE B: "Good morning. I'm so sorry for my delay in getting back to you. Please accept my apology. I agree, I think it looks great, thank you."

In the first text, we're hearing from a person who feels she has the power. She doesn't take ownership of the delay or, for that matter, offer an apology. Rather, she instructs the recipient to do something for her—forgive the delay. There's a substantive difference between "I'm so sorry" and "Forgive the delay." "I'm so sorry" takes ownership of the harm caused, whereas "Forgive the delay" (without adding "I'm sorry") is nothing more than a request of the other person with zero acknowledgment of personal wrongdoing.

Let's take another example. Turning down the hallway, Person A bumps into an innocent and jolted Person B, of equal professional status. Person A says, "I'm sorry," and Person B says, "Excuse me." "Excuse me" is passive rather than active (diluting ownership); it puts the self second (outwardly focused) and makes a request of the listener— "I want you to do something for me: to excuse me" (a tacit signal of power). Further proof is that you can facetiously say, "Excuse me!" because it is an innately inauthentic apology. In contrast, "I'm sorry" cannot be said mockingly—barring extreme theatrics—because the active voice and the "I" ownership inherently convey sincerity.[6]

Although either phasing is proper and preferred over "Watch where you're going, buster," each hallway muttering reveals something about the individual's personality—assuming a pattern of this syntax—and the relationship dynamic. Either Person A is more willing to assume personal responsibility for his actions (an indication of good mental health) or he may suffer from feelings of inferiority and is quick to take blame (an indication of poor mental health). We can't gauge either person's emotional health based on this exchange, but if we knew a little more about

> Observe any two people speaking, even when you can't hear what they are saying, and the one who is pointing is the one with the power (or who feels empowered because he believes he holds the higher moral ground).

each person's station in life, we'd learn much more from this simple interaction.

Should this same scene unfold with a four-star general bumping into a new cadet, we might be surprised to hear the general say, "I'm sorry," and the cadet offer up, "Excuse me." The focus of an emotionally healthy cadet should move reflexively inward to produce a self-focused apology, such as "I'm so sorry." But again, not always. "Excuse me, sir" might also be appropriate and, once again, may foreshadow something about the cadet. Yet if we up the ante, whereby the cadet spills his drink on the general, then "Excuse me, sir" no longer suffices. We would expect an effusive first-person apology from the cadet, and its absence points to his warped perception of status and invites inquiry into his emotional health.

We can also rely on a strikingly accurate visual cue: the direction of someone's head tilt. When a person feels ashamed because of his actions or rebuke, you'll note that his head tilts slightly downward. It's an indication that he is contrite—signaling submission. If, however, his chin tilts upward, he is feeling defiant and is unlikely to back down apologetically.[7] You'll notice this instinctual reaction with children. When a small child is chastised, his head goes down. Similarly, in response to a false assumption or accusation, most emotionally healthy adults will display a slight head tilt upward, indicating that they have taken offense, as if to say, "What are you talking about?"

In part III we will return to our accident-prone cadet and discover how personality types and pathologies are observed through interactions not only with other people but also with inanimate objects—because there is quite a difference between the person who says, "I can't open the window"; the one who says, "The window is stuck"; and the one who says, "The window is broken." Up next, we will continue to learn how to read a person within a specific situation itself. Here you'll discover what calm and confidence look like and how anger and anxiety leak out in subtle ways.

CHAPTER 5

Reading the Mood

An athlete or artist who is "in the zone" is flawless in her performance because when she is absorbed in an objective her attention is solely on what needs to be done. Likewise, a confident person is able to focus outwardly on the objective, and the "I" disappears (just as the linguistic "I" does).

Of course, sometimes it makes sense to be hyperfocused on yourself. Note how you usually take the first sip from a hot, steaming cup of coffee or tea. Your level of concentration is intense. You move slowly, watching the cup as it comes to your lips, and then haltingly, hesitatingly taste the brew. Your behavior indicates the stakes. As interest increases (in this instance, not wanting to scald oneself), a chain reaction ensues: confidence decreases (as the risk is greater), perspective narrows (as the ego engages and we become fearful), and anxiety increases (because the ego needs to feel in control). This chain reaction isn't specific to hot beverages. If you know what to look for, confidence (or the lack thereof) is easy to spot.

The Psychology of Confidence

If you were asked to walk along a wide painted line on the floor, you would do so with complete ease. You might glance down to get your bearings only to look up and around as you move across the room. You'd probably check a ringing phone and speak or joke with abandon. Asked to do the same task on a narrower line, your attention would increase significantly. Now take the same thin line and place it on a plank twenty stories high. You would walk slowly, paying attention to each step and focusing on nothing else, certainly not using the phone or taking in the view. You would be entirely self-focused because of the higher stakes of physical safety.[1] The same thing is true of emotional safety.

How can you tell who feels like they are walking on the ground and who feels like they are twenty feet in the air? The person paying more attention to himself is the one who feels more anxious. Let's look more deeply at the process. There are four stages to a person's actions:

1. **Unconscious incompetence** is when a person is unaware that he is not performing correctly.
2. **Conscious incompetence** is when a person is aware that he has not acquired the skill set necessary to be as effective and successful as he would like to be.
3. **Conscious competence** is when a person is aware of what he needs to do, but awareness is needed in order to be effective.
4. **Unconscious competence** is when a person can perform correctly and as necessary without his full, or even partial, attention.

Learning to drive a stick shift car effectively illustrates the four levels. At first it feels completely foreign, but the driver eventually has the skill to shift gears without consciously focusing on what she is doing;

the process is now integrated into muscle memory and can be instinctually performed. Muscle memory is related to procedural memory, which is a type of unconscious long-term memory that helps us perform specific tasks with minimal attention; we can automatically access procedural memories without conscious awareness.

Similarly, note the contrast between a new driver and a seasoned pro. The former gets behind the wheel and checks everything. His gaze locks onto the gear shift as he puts the car into reverse. His head tilts downward as he slowly releases the clutch and puts his foot on the gas. One thing at a time. There is no buckling the seatbelt while backing up or twisting open the cap of a soft drink while steering with his knee. But what happens to our seasoned driver when we introduce a stressor— a snowstorm with zero visibility? He turns off the radio. His hands grip the wheel at the recommended position of eight o'clock and four o'clock. Psychologically, higher stakes narrow our perspective, increase our anxiety, and reorient our focus.

During a casual conversation with an employee, you notice they reach for a can of soda well within their grasp. They watch their hand extend to the drink. Then they watch their hand as it moves the can up to their lips. Your employee is feeling insecure and does not trust themselves to do what they have done hundreds of thousands of times previously without paying attention. This shows a higher level of anxiety than a casual and presumably friendly encounter would indicate. Whether in a meeting, on a date, or in an interrogation, the person who feels nervous is hyperaware of everything they say and do. Their demeanor may be stiff; their movements and gestures, awkward and mechanical. What were once unconscious actions become part of a heightened state of awareness.

> Psychologically, higher stakes narrow our perspective, increase our anxiety, and reorient our focus.

The Anxious Tells

If you've ever blanked in a moment of stress or choked under pressure, increased self-focus is the culprit. A normally automatic or unconscious activity is disrupted by consciousness of it or reflection on it, and as the stakes get higher, the anxiety increases, and our cognitive faculties become increasingly compromised. The result? Performance suffers.

Because anxiety shifts our focus to the self, our ability to absorb new information is also diminished. Have you ever met someone at a party and forgotten her name right after you were introduced? Likewise, when we are nervous, we take things more literally; our brain is busy scanning for observable threats, and while it tries to get its bearings, we often cannot process other information beyond a superficial level. In the face of any threat—physical or emotional—we are on high alert, and the cognitive resources required to make tangential connections are diverted elsewhere.

Accordingly, in the face of a threat, we often have trouble processing humor, particularly sarcasm. To recognize a sarcastic comment, we have to perceive the contradiction between the surface level (literal) meaning and the intended meaning.[2] The *prefrontal cortex* (the thinking brain) is required to integrate the literal meaning with the speaker's intended message. Because anxiety or anger causes the brain to engage the more primitive *amygdala* (the emotion response center), our response time is slowed. We first have to bring the thinking brain back online before we can understand the connotation or inference. What does this look like in real life? The anxious person misses the sarcasm and stares blankly or laughs nervously before catching on.

Physical Manifestations of Anxiety

Self-conscious manifestations also include fidgeting, touching our face and hair, picking at our skin, rubbing our leg, and playing with our fingers. Watch for the following signs of intense anxiety or fear:

- A person's face becoming flushed or turning white from extreme fear. Look for rapid breathing and increased perspiration. In addition, take note of whether he is trying to control his breathing to calm himself. His efforts to remain calm will appear as deep, audible inhaling and exhaling.
- Trembling or shaking in voice or body. His hands may tremble. If he's hiding his hands, it might be an attempt to hide uncontrollable shaking. His voice may crack and seem inconsistent.
- Difficulty swallowing—hence the expression "all choked up." Television or movie actors who wish to express fear or sadness often use this behavior. Throat clearing is also a sign of nervousness. Anxiety causes mucus to form in the throat. A public speaker who is nervous often clears his throat before speaking.
- Vocal changes. Vocal cords, like all muscles, tighten when a person is stressed, producing a higher sound, octave, or pitch.

The Language of Anxiety

Because emotional distress orients our attention inward, the frequent use of personal pronouns is a hallmark of an anxious state. Not all pronouns are created equal. The personal pronoun *me* indicates inward orientation, as does the pronoun *I*, but because it almost always is used in a passive tense—whereby something acts on the person rather than the person taking action—*me* is indicative of feelings of helplessness and vulnerability; and when *me* is used superfluously, the anxiety rings ever more loudly. For instance:

"My stomach hurts" versus "My stomach hurts me."
"Why are you yelling?" versus "Why are you yelling at me?"

Because anxiety and anger are inextricably linked, an angry state is also associated with *me*-language. In both states, the person sees himself as a victim, triggering him to use *me*-language (e.g., "How could you do this to me?").

An anxious state is also easy to spot by the frequent use of *qualifiers*, which are expressions of uncertainty or indecisiveness (e.g., "I think"; "I wonder"; "I guess"). The use of qualifiers increases with a person's anxiety and usually come before the completed verb, diluting a speaker's conviction in her statement.[3] When you know something is true, you do not find it necessary to buttress your confidence to either yourself or another person. For example, barring an existentialist dilemma, you would not say, "I believe I exist." You know you exist and therefore state the truism without qualification: "I exist." Imagine you're suffering from an uncomfortable skin rash and make your way to the dermatologist. After a thorough exam, she hands you a prescription and says either "This medication will help" or "I think this medication will help." Which would you rather hear? Qualifiers erode conviction rather than reinforce it.

All this said, it is only when expressing subjective—not objective—information (e.g., an opinion, preference, or desire) that the use of a qualifier signals insecurity or uncertainty (see chapter 10 for elaboration). The challenge in decoding the syntax is further complicated by repressed anxiety. We will see later that narcissists, for example, compensate for deep-seated insecurities with definitive, rather than tentative, speech.

A *state* is a temporary way of feeling; it reflects our thoughts or responses to the current situation. A *trait* is a more stable characteristic or pattern of thoughts, feelings, and behaviors, and thus serves as a valuable predictor of future behavior.

To accurately detect a person in an anxious state, you will want to observe a qualifier in conjunction with another marker: a linguistic *retractor* (e.g., *but, although, however, nevertheless*). This language pattern cements the presence of anxiety because, like qualifiers, retractors speak to tentativeness—the former, before the action; the latter, after the action.[4] Retractors and qualifiers disclose deliberation and indecision. Effectively they are laying an escape plan into any forward movement (e.g., "I think that this could be okay, but I don't know"; "I guess it might make sense, so I could try it, although . . ."). This indicates not only a state of anxiety but also the possible presence of its blood relative, trait obsessiveness and fear of vulnerability, risk, or failure. Additionally, negations (e.g., *no, not, never*) and negativity (e.g., *fail, bad, poor*) are associated with increased anxiety and insecurity. The same situation can be framed either through a positive or negative lens. In other words, a person who says, "There's a chance it may work" or "It's possible we may succeed," likely feels more confident (or has less at stake) than one who says, "This will probably fail" or "It's not likely to work."

It's important to distinguish traits from states. In other words, you want to determine whether someone is behaving a certain way because of who they are at the core or whether they're simply reacting to a particular situation. A *state* is a temporary way of feeling; it reflects our thoughts or responses to the current situation. A *trait* is a more stable characteristic or pattern of thoughts, feelings, and behaviors and thus serves as a valuable predictor of future behavior. Someone with an anxiety trait, for instance, is primed to perceive a "safe" situation as threatening and is predisposed to react with heightened and disproportionate anxiety.[5] Intuitively, a person who worries a lot over trivial matters (trait) is more likely to become tense in any given situation (state).[6]

To confirm whether you are observing a trait or a state (or both), we want to now take note of frequency, duration, intensity, and context. More on this in parts III and IV.

Poker Corner

Nervous betting often accompanies a strong hand because the player feels a great deal of tension. ("This is it, big-time!") He has to make sure that he capitalizes on it and doesn't choke. Interestingly, and counterintuitively, a person who is bluffing will often appear more casual for two reasons: First, he is managing his impression and wants to make sure that he comes off as nonchalant and unworried; but second, and more psychologically profound, he is in control. He can bet, raise, or fold. He makes the choice to bluff, and this control makes him feel more confident. The person with a strong hand has no legitimate choice other than *betting, seeing,* or *raising.* He can't fold, so the pressure is felt more intensely, not less so.

Fear Leads to Anger

The lower our self-esteem in general—and how much the uncomfortable truth affects our self-image in particular—the more fearful we become. The ego tells us that we are vulnerable and in danger. Enter the *fight-flight-freeze response,* which is a physiological reaction to a perceived threat—physical or emotional. The sympathetic nervous system activates the adrenal glands, which release adrenaline, noradrenaline, and cortisol into the bloodstream. This injection reroutes the body's reaction from the prefrontal cortex to the amygdala. A person who gets angry is, to some extent, fearful. The response to fear—the ego's attempt to compensate for the loss—is anger. Anger provides the illusion of control because, physiologically, the release of these substances increases awareness, energy, and strength. Emotionally, anger directs our attention away from ourselves, which also mimics the sensation that we are more secure. Let's look at a diverse set of circumstances that can lead to anger and see how the process unfolds in a consistently similar way:[7]

- Someone cuts you off on the road. (catalyst) → You lose control of the situation, as you had to swerve or hit your brakes in order to avoid an accident. → This causes you to become scared, thinking of "what might have happened." → You then direct anger at the other driver.
- Your child refuses to wear her warm jacket. (catalyst) → You feel that you are not in control of the situation. → You may become fearful that she does not respect you and will not listen to other things that you ask her to do. → You then become angry with her for not listening to you.
- A person is rude to you. (catalyst) → Depending on who it is, this act of disrespect may cause you to doubt yourself. → To some extent, you may become fearful that he doesn't like or respect you, and this causes you to question your own self-worth and image. → You become angry because the way you wish for others to treat and relate to you is different from how the situation is evolving.

Our need to feel in control also extends to situations that have nothing to do with other people. For instance:

- You trip over a chair in the dark. (catalyst) → You lose control, meaning that your plan to walk from point A to point B without tripping was disrupted. → This causes you to become scared, as you may have injured yourself. → You then become angry. (Interestingly, some people become angry at themselves, at the chair—kicking it—or even at the person who put it there for you to trip over.)

Logically, anger offers no real satisfaction or psychological comfort. It is our ego's defense mechanism to feeling vulnerable, yet we spiral out of control and become emotionally weaker with each intense anger-driven thought or action.

The Language of Anger

He says he's furious, but it may all be a show. She wrote to you that everything is fine, but you think she is secretly seething. Planning. Plotting. Even when a person is angry, it doesn't mean that he comes out swinging. An individual's unique personality will dictate his modus operandi.[8]

Assertive-aggressive (fight): He comes out fighting to control the situation (you) overtly. He knows that he's angry and isn't afraid to show it.

Passive-aggressive (fight-flight): His anger leaks out in subtle ways. He knows he is angry but can't handle confrontation. Unable to confront directly, he seeks control stealthily.

Suppression (flight): He doesn't consciously acknowledge his anger, so he controls it by suppressing his emotions and telling himself that he isn't angry at all.

Immobilization (freeze): He buries the anger. Feeling powerless, he closes down and insulates himself from the pain. He thinks, *I can shut out the world. I will be safe. I will be in control.*

Surrender (flight): He either tells himself that he isn't worthy of asserting himself or that it's just not worth it.

Grammatically speaking, an angry state is distinguished by the use of more second- and third-person pronouns.[9] Remember, the first person is the "I" (*me, my, mine, myself*) perspective. The second person is the "you" (*your, yours, yourself*) perspective. The third person is the "he/she/it/they" (*his, himself, hers, herself, their, themselves*) perspective.

A pronoun shift (from first to second and third person) makes perfect sense when you're angry. Emotionally, anger serves to channel, mask, or otherwise redirect our attention away from ourselves. The language we use follows the same path: Moving away from "I" and toward "you" notably predicts hostility (and linguistic self-defense or deflection) and signals the state of anger.[10]

Counterintuitively, an angry state does produce *me*-language, even though the pronoun *I* is used less frequently. While the pronoun *me* is typically used to express passivity (whereby something or someone "acted upon me"), an angry person sees himself as a victim (of some force) and thus is an object of unfair and undeserved mistreatment (e.g., "How dare you do this to me?"; "How could this be happening to me?"). Subsequently, an angry person will ask more (rhetorical) questions. These often occur in the form of rhetorical phrases (e.g., "What is your problem?"; "What are you doing to me?"; "Where'd you learn how to type?"). In this state, a person will also use fewer cooperative pronouns (such as *we, us,* and *our*), more swear words, and more negations (e.g., *no, not, never*) and negativity (e.g., *fail, loss, hate*).[11]

Overt anger (assertive-aggressive) is easy to recognize. When someone is screaming or scolding you, it's clear how they are feeling. But anger is not always expressed. Indeed, sometimes it is suppressed (conscious blocking of unwanted thoughts or impulses) or repressed (unconscious blocking) altogether. An absence of qualifiers and retractors, an increase in concrete nouns, and a decrease in function words are reliable indicators of latent hostility. Because anger engages to embolden us, its language must be absolute and definitive. Think bold colors, not pastels. If qualifiers and retractors define an anxious state, their absence identifies an angry state. Linguistic analysis shows a decreased use of both qualifiers and retractors by a latently hostile person. Note how the first statement below strikes an authentic note, while the second one feels middling, almost comical.

STATEMENT A: I'm furious with you for even thinking you could steal from me.

STATEMENT B: I believe [qualifier] I'm furious with you for even thinking you could do that to me, although [retractor] . . .

Unqualified language also means an increase in the use of concrete nouns and a decrease in function words.[12] An angry person uses direct and unequivocal language because she does not want any misunderstanding; this means sentences with exact pronouns and proper nouns (i.e., names and places)—for example, "I told Jim three times not to let the accountant into the executive suite" rather than "I told him a few times not to let him back here." The meaning of the first sentence is unambiguous and does not rely on shared knowledge or perspective.

> An absence of qualifiers and retractors, an increase in concrete nouns, and a decrease in function words are reliable indicators of latent hostility.

As we learned, in an angry state, the ego is fully engaged. Just as our language does not contain the words *us* and *we*, we do not want to connect or share anything with the person or object of our disdain. No matter how calmly spoken or how delicately written with smiley-face emoticons, there is an assumption of latent anger or at least bubbling frustration within the situation.

In face-to-face interactions, be aware that a smile is the most common mask for emotion because it best conceals the appearance in the lower face of anger, disgust, sadness, or fear. In other words, a person who doesn't want her true feelings to be exposed may "put on a happy face." A smile that's genuine lights up the whole face. When a smile is forced, the person's mouth is closed and tight and there's no movement in the eyes or forehead. This is similar to that of someone who is embarrassed by a joke but wants to pretend that she thinks it's funny. What you see is a "lips only" smile, not a big grin encompassing her entire face.

As we learned throughout part I, when it comes to thoughts and feelings, the emotional landscape regarding intention is not always clear. A person may be sincere even though they're feeling insecure. Or they do not think they are lying to you, because in actuality they are lying to themselves and believe what they say. In part II, the stakes are higher and the tactics sharper because it's crystal clear. Here, it's you against them. And the question is: Is this someone who will give you the shirt off his back, or, if given the chance, will he look to stab you in the back?

PART II

THE HUMAN LIE DETECTOR

Are you dealing with a really bad guy? A master manipulator or an outright con artist? In the chapters that follow, you'll learn how to easily tell whether someone is out for you or to get you. Protect yourself and your loved ones—emotionally, financially, and physically—from people who will lie, cheat, and steal to get their way into your hearts and pocketbooks. With these techniques, you will never be fooled, lied to, or taken advantage of again.

CHAPTER 6

Assessing Honesty and Integrity

Whenever you're speaking to a person with questionable motives, you should ask yourself: Is this someone who is likely to open up to me and be willing to have an honest conversation, or does he have a trick or two up his sleeve? To find out, we'll begin with a look at game theory and the ultimatum game, created by the Israeli economist Ariel Rubinstein.

Rubinstein offered random strangers the opportunity to participate in a game in which two people interacted only once and completely anonymously. Each pair was given one hundred dollars, but the twist was that one person (of the pair) was arbitrarily chosen to divide the money any way they chose. The receiving partner could either accept or reject the offer. If the offer was accepted, they would divide the money accordingly, and if rejected, both would leave empty-handed.[1] Rubinstein accurately predicted that the person who got to decide how to distribute the money in such a game would more often than not offer the other person less than they would keep themselves; the split was rarely generous. No real surprise here. What is intriguing is that subsequent studies revealed how to predict the likelihood that the receiver would accept the offer—or, in a word, cooperate—by the observation of a single behavior.

Researchers videotaped the receivers' facial expressions as they faced unfair offers, and analysis found that cooperators—those who accepted the offer—displayed more emotional expression when responding to unfair offers.[2] In other words, if they didn't like the offer, they wouldn't mask their dissatisfaction with a poker face or "put on a happy face." They showed their dissatisfaction even when they ultimately accepted the offer.[3] The study concluded that emotional expressiveness is a strong indication of both cooperation and trustworthiness.[4]

This study led me and my team to field-test a hypothesis about another way to gauge whether a person is likely to be cooperative. Here's what we found with uncanny accuracy: When a person narrates her present behavior, it is a strong indication that she wants to have an open discussion. For example, a coworker comes into your office and, as she gets herself comfortable, voices aloud, "Let me just get myself situated," "Okay, let me sit down," or "I'm just going to open up this drink." Although it is patently obvious what she is doing, the narration indicates a desire for transparency and connection, which is consistent with a cooperative, rather than confrontational, disposition.[5]

Similarly, take note how a parent, teacher, or babysitter engages a small child in play. Narration is usually present because the adult seeks a connection with the child. "Let's open up the box . . . Ooh, what do we have here? It squeaks when I push on its belly!" Intuitively, we pick up that the adult is trying to bond with the child. Imagine watching a scene whereby the adult silently takes out the toys and sets everything up without speaking aloud. Unless the adult is trying to build suspense to surprise the child, it strikes us as a little cold. Distant.

Because self-narration requires us to feel comfortable in our surroundings, there are times when it

> When a person narrates her present behavior, it is a strong indication that she wants to have an open discussion.

would seem out of place and thus suspicious. You don't have be in law enforcement to recognize just how odd it would be for a suspect—no matter how innocent—to engage in self-narration upon walking into the police station: "Okay, Detective, let me just take off my jacket and get settled in." Although we expect the innocent person to become more open in conversation, he is justifiably guarded at the point of initial contact.

Nonverbal Cluster Bombs

You can readily see how comfortable someone is with a particular topic by paying attention to how she navigates the physical space between the two of you. We naturally sit closer or lean toward whomever we want to connect with. If someone feels uncomfortable or is uninterested, however, she might angle her body toward the exit or actually move in that direction. While standing, she may position her back to the wall. Note whether she uses inanimate objects (e.g., a cushion, a vase, anything) to form a barrier between you and her. Placing such a barrier is the verbal equivalent of "I don't want to talk about it." Since she can't get up and leave, her displeasure manifests itself in the formation of physical barriers between her and the source of the discomfort.

In much the same way that we physically hide our eyes and emotionally conceal our "I"s when we lie, we also tend to adopt a more defensive and nonexpressive posture. The red meat of typical body language clues informs us that open postures and gestures indicate confidence.

When people sit with their legs and arms close to their body, they may be echoing the thought *I'm keeping something in*. When we feel comfortable and confident, we tend to stretch out—to claim our space, as it were. When we feel less secure, we fold our arms and legs into our body, occupying less physical space.

Introducing a Stressor

All of the above is true. But body language is also too easy to fake and altogether impractical to gauge when you're not face-to-face. In order to upgrade your read, you'll need to turn up the heat slightly by introducing an emotional stressor.[6] The objective here is to ask a question or make a statement that does not accuse the person of anything but alludes to the possible behavior. If he doesn't realize you're implying anything, then he's probably not hiding anything. But if he gets defensive, then he knows what you're getting at and the only way he could know is if he is guilty of the charge.

> SUSPICION: A transportation supervisor suspects that a bus driver was drinking while on duty.

> QUESTION: "John, I'd like to get your advice on something. A colleague of mine at another terminal has a problem with one of her drivers. She feels he may be drinking while on duty. Do you have any suggestions on how she can approach the driver about this problem?"

If he's guilty, he'll become uncomfortable. If he's not drinking on the job, then he will be pleased that his advice was sought out and offer his opinion. Answers such as "Did someone say something to you?" or "Why are you asking me about this?" indicate concern on the employee's part. This doesn't mean that he's definitely guilty, but you may want to turn up the heat even more. You do this by making an accusation, which then puts the person directly on the defensive.

Responding to an Accusation

As a general guideline, a truthful response is short and direct, not convoluted, long-winded, or complicated. When someone doesn't deny the allegations against him—or when he buries a "no" under two pages of musings or a ten-minute diatribe—this is a strong indication of deception. A reliable denial is direct and clear (e.g., "No, I didn't do it"). If, however, the denial consists of statements like "How could you even ask me such a thing?" or "This is crazy!" or "Ask anyone who knows me, I would never do that!" or "How could you question my honesty?" then that raises suspicions, not so much because of the person's vociferousness but because none of these responses consists of a direct, straightforward denial. People falsely accused, who are providing true statements, have no reason to hold back from strong, clear denials. People being deceptive, while certainly aiming to distance themselves from guilt, often have difficulty with using direct, unambiguous language in their denial.

The bottom line is that if someone didn't kill his wife, then you don't want to hear that he loved his wife and he would never do that or that he's not a monster or a crazy person. If a teacher didn't abuse his student, you don't want to hear that he would never harm a child or that he's not a pervert or that everyone in the school loves him. If your employee didn't steal from your company or your nanny didn't harm your child, you don't want to hear from her that "everyone loves me . . . my reputation is spotless . . . I am not a bad person." All of this may be good and true—and it's fine if such denials are included in a full response to an accusation (after the direct denial)—but the centerpiece of the person's response should be a consistent, clear *denial of the act* and *not proof that he is not the kind of person who could ever commit such an act.*[7]

And while we're on the subject of denials, keep in mind that not all denials are created equal. A statement such as, "I deny these allegations" is not the same as "I didn't do it." A denial of an allegation means that the person is refusing to acknowledge guilt, but this is not the same as denying the behavior. A reliable denial is a clear "no." Only *no* is a "no," and, for that matter, only *yes* is a "yes."

Along these lines, a lack of candor is indicated when someone stalls because she needs to buy herself time to consider her options, prepare her answer, or shift the topic entirely. Therefore, she might ask you to repeat the question, repeat the question herself, ask you to qualify the question, qualify her own answer, or answer your question with a question. For example, when you're interviewing a potential babysitter, you might ask, "Have you ever hit a child in your care?" Here are what red-flag responses sound like:

"That's a good question" or "I'm glad you asked that."
"To be perfectly honest," "to be frank," or "to tell you the truth."
"Well, it's not as simple as yes or no."
"You know I'm against that sort of thing. I think it's morally
    reprehensible."

Also included in this category is the ever-pervasive and always annoying response: "Why would I lie to you?" If you get this response to an accusation you've made, be suspicious. If someone's being accused of something he's done, then he probably has an excellent reason to lie. In just about any situation, if you feel that you're being lied to, it is often best not to confront the person immediately. If you're wrong, you may injure the relationship and cause the person to instantly go on the defense, making it difficult to gather more information.

The Energy of Lies

Because telling a lie requires more mental energy than telling the truth, liars often resort to shortcuts—meaning they express themselves in a way that minimizes the need for deep thought and reflection. So be aware of the following four telltale signs of deceit, because if you hear or read one or more of these signs, you might have good reason to be concerned:

- Pontificating and philosophizing
- Self-referral statements

- The complexity of simplicity
- Relief after the conversation

Pontificating and Philosophizing

Any statement, written or verbal, that begins to expound on a sense of fairness or justice can be problematic, unless the person is actually confessing, in which case such declarations would be expected. Pay attention to philosophical departures, which can include anything from "It shouldn't be this way" to "Kids these days don't understand" to "This is not the country I remember." The psychology behind pontificating or getting philosophical is that unconsciously the person is looking for internal justification for her behavior—and validation from you—all the while seeking to present herself as a moral and just person with good, wholesome values and ideals.

Self-Referral Statements

A self-referral statement, where the person refers back to her own words, is also a red flag. In writing, people use phrases such as "As I wrote above," "As previously mentioned," and "As explained earlier," to avoid relaying incorrect information, and because it takes more brain power to lie. It is just plain easier to refer back to what was previously said than to tell the lie again. In conversation, the same thing occurs. You may hear the overuse of such phrases as "As I said previously," or "I answered that

> Because telling a lie requires more mental energy than telling the truth, liars often resort to shortcuts—meaning they express themselves in a way that minimizes the need for deep thought and reflection.

before." In general, a liar is more likely to repeat words and phrases in order to keep her story streamlined and to reduce the cognitive load.[8]

The Complexity of Simplicity

Honest statements and truthful expressions typically use a more complex sentence structure because to be accurate we need to make distinctions—using words such as *except, without, but,* or *apart from.* A person who is lying has a more difficult time with these words because it is cognitively draining to keep track of what he did not do and what did not happen while relaying what he did do and what did happen.

Let's take an example of a product review. The more truthful the review, the more likely it will contain longer and more complex sentences. Why? Because the reviewer is qualifying his opinion to ensure honesty, which means that the product is not "the best thing since sliced bread"; rather, "it is, in many ways, the best thing since sliced bread, except for the XYZ feature, which feels outdated." Bear in mind a critical distinction. Liars tend to use longer and more *convoluted,* but not *complex,* wording. Their sentences meander and are stuffed with insignificant details and non sequiturs, whereas truth tellers communicate with sentences that are clear and generally direct, even with a complex structure.

Relief after the Conversation

Because deception takes energy, watch and listen carefully during a conversation when the subject is changed. Does the person become happier? Does he seem more relaxed? He might even offer a smile or a nervous laugh. Notice his posture. Does it become more relaxed and less defensive? The giveaway here is how fast and dramatically his mood changes, indicating his discomfort with the previous subject matter. Test him to see whether he's quick to change the subject. If he has been accused of something downright awful and is innocent, he will resent the accusations and insist that the topic be explored further—either now, if possible, or in the immediate future, and he will indicate not just willingness but a strong desire to do so. The guilty person wants the subject changed and the conversation to end; the innocent person always wants a further exchange of information.

Although isolated body language signs are notoriously unreliable, particularly those that are easily controlled, an often overlooked opportunity emerges—not in spite of the ease with which we can manage our body language but because of it. In the next chapter, we learn how the posture and posturing of a person in both *guarded* and *unguarded* exchanges provides us with a window into his real position and plans.

> The guilty person wants the subject changed and the conversation to end; the innocent person always wants a further exchange of information.

CHAPTER 7

The Art of Reading the Bluff

The influential psychologist William James writes, "We don't laugh because we're happy, we're happy because we laugh." Extensive research shows that body language not only reflects but also affects our thoughts, feelings, and behaviors. The mind and body work together to form what is called *embodied cognition,* which explains that how we hold ourselves— our physical posture, poses, and gestures—produces a wide range of near-instantaneous cognitive and behavioral changes. In one study, participants were randomly assigned to adopt open, expansive postures (spread-out limbs and more occupied space) or to assume closed, constricted postures. Those who adopted the expansive poses for just sixty seconds not only felt more powerful and self-confident but acted in a manner consistent with the effect of power and demonstrated a greater willingness to take action.[1] In another experiment, randomly assigned subjects were asked to sit either slumped in their seats or straight up while filling out a mock job application. When asked for an honest self-evaluation, those in the latter group rated themselves more competent and capable than their slouching counterparts did.[2]

In casual observations, a person's confidence level may be observed through his overall demeanor. This is because we can assume congruency with his thoughts. In other words, if he's looking down, he's probably feeling down. But I have to stress that this applies *only* to unguarded observations or interactions. This does not work in any situation where a person recognizes that he is being watched—such as in a negotiation or in any power struggle—because he may be putting on a show. Body language cues are typically misleading when it comes to guarded interactions. It is, however, exactly for this reason that we gain a powerful advantage. Let's look at the psychology through the lens of technology.

Apple's Mistake

When the Apple iPod was first introduced, it came with a nifty feature called "shuffle." In this mode, songs would be played randomly from our preset playlist. The problem is that true randomness doesn't always seem so random, and listeners were treated to the same song playing back-to-back or to certain songs in heavy rotation while, at least in the short run, other songs received little or no play time. When flipping a coin, the likelihood of an even distribution of heads and tails emerges over time, but we could also get a run of heads or tails, making it seem as if something is wrong. Apple then introduced a new algorithm to make the playlist appear more random—and play songs according to our assumption of randomness. This was a helpful innovation when it came to hearing all the playlist, but buyer beware: The perfectly even distribution of songs is the giveaway that the randomness is faked.

Poker Corner

The gambler makes a big mistake if he believes that if an event occurs more frequently than normal during a given period, it will occur less frequently in the future. (There's even a clinical term for this mindset: *the gambler's fallacy*). Or, put another way, he would be mistaken to think that random events are more or less likely to occur because of the frequency that they have occurred in the past. For instance, if you flip a coin five times and it lands on heads each time, you might think that the coin is *due* to land on tails. However, because each event is independent, the likelihood of it landing on either heads or tails is 50/50 *every time you flip it*, independent of the number of heads or tails that have come before. In poker, a player would be quite disinclined to bluff after winning a huge pot because he would assume that the other players would not believe his good fortune—to have two great winning hands back-to-back—and would call his bluff because he was *due* for a losing hand.[3]

This brings us to the conundrum for someone who is bluffing. Not unlike Apple, the bluffer has to simulate what authenticity looks and sounds like. The giveaway is that much like true randomness, the truth doesn't always sound truthful. Let me explain the psychology: Let's say you show someone some highly disturbing photographs of a crime scene and she doesn't show much reaction. You might surmise that the woman lacks empathy and decency and is more likely to be guilty of the crime herself. It is precisely for this reason, however, that the guilty person will almost always show his disgust. In his mind, that is what good, normal people do when they are shown revolting pictures. This is not to say that an innocent person would not react similarly, only that she would not feel it necessary to do so.

Let's take another example. A couple is told that their young daughter is missing. They are distraught and may blame each other or themselves (e.g., "I shouldn't have let her go to that friend's house"; "Why did I drop her off by herself?"). These exclamations point to innocence, not guilt. Guilty people rarely claim any responsibility because *they are guilty.* In their mind, the last thing they think they should do is put up a neon sign pointing to themselves. Alas, innocent people do not hide their feelings of guilt or blame. They are quick to beat themselves up for what they could or should have done differently.

With this awareness, we are now able to detect a bluff through *impression management* and the universal mistake that almost everyone makes.[4]

In Guarded Exchanges

Sun Tzu, in *The Art of War*, neatly distills the bluff: If able, appear unable; if active, appear inactive; if near, appear far; if far, appear near. When a person is bluffing, he is managing others' impression of him to convey the "right" effect and serve whatever agenda he has. Conversely, the authentic person is not interested in how he is coming across. He is unconcerned with his image, unlike his deceptive counterpart, who focuses solely on others' impressions of him and puts a great deal of effort into presenting a certain image. The thing about it is that he almost always goes too far. His algorithm is off.

A bluff occurs when someone is really against something but pretends to be for it—or when he is for something and pretends to be against it. Consequently, when a person bluffs, he usually tries to appear as if he doesn't care when he really does, and he pretends to be concerned when he really isn't. In any case, he is trying to create a false impression to disguise his true intentions. Therein lies the key: People who bluff habitually overcompensate, in either direction, and you can uncover a bluff instantly by noticing how someone tries to appear.

Poker Corner

A card player bets heavily and raises the pot. Does he have the cards or simply guts? When a person is bluffing in a poker hand, he wants to show he is not timid. He might put his money in quickly. But if he does have a good hand, what might he do? He may deliberate a bit, putting it in slowly, showing he is not really sure about his hand. Poker professionals know that a bluffing person will give the impression he has a strong hand, while the person with a strong hand will often give the impression that his hand is weak.

A partner in a law firm says he's going to leave unless he is allowed to take on a certain case. Is it a hollow threat or the real deal? If it were genuine, he likely would not make a point of trying to convey his confidence. However, we can easily observe an air of overconfidence if he is bluffing. This is, of course, because we have to assume that since he's at the firm, he wants to be there. And that he will be "forced" to leave only if he doesn't get what he's asking for. Logic dictates that he would rather stay and get the case than not get it and leave. If he thus appears overly committed to the idea of leaving if he doesn't get the case, you can assume he's bluffing—because we know that he really doesn't want to leave but is trying to create that impression.

"The lady doth protest too much, methinks" is a line from William Shakespeare's *Hamlet,* spoken by Queen Gertrude when she observed the insincere overacting of a character in the play within the play. It implies that a person who proclaims something too fiercely is hiding the truth. People might put up a strong front because they know they will crumble if they ever have to defend their position. It has been said that the easiest people to sell to are those who have a sign saying, "No salesmen or solicitors." The reasoning is that these people know deep down that if a salesman does get to them, they will buy whatever he has to sell.

Similarly, if the attorney is sincere in his stance that he will leave if he doesn't get his way, then he will appear reluctant, even conflicted. He will use phrases like "I'm sorry, this is what I need to make this work" or "I'm afraid there's not a whole lot of room for negotiation here." This person's words provide comfort for his opponent, not a shield for himself.

> People who bluff habitually overcompensate, in either direction, and you can uncover a bluff instantly by noticing how someone tries to appear.

You shouldn't have to sell the truth; it should speak for itself. Halloween displays with *Boo* and *Scary* do not frighten anyone. If you're old enough to read the words, you realize that they are a poor substitute for the intended impact. Declarations of emphasis, called *oversell expressions,* often indicate active impression management. Consider the suspect who says that he is "100 percent not guilty" or is "absolutely, completely positive that . . ." People often inject such words with the intention to present an image of confidence, but if I asked whether you had ever robbed a bank, you would likely respond with "No," and not "I am certain I never robbed a bank" or "I promise I never robbed a bank."

The person who is not bluffing is typically more solemn—and less prone to become emotional. In the case of our attorney, if he is not bluffing, then he knows that he will have to leave if it comes down to it. But if he is bluffing, it won't come down to anything because he's not leaving! The attitudes of both people are completely different and make it clear whether it's a bluff or the real thing. Follow the logic. A typical threat indicates that the person would rather not follow through on it because he still wants something else, something more. Otherwise, he would simply carry out the threat without warning you of it. In other words, a person who says, "You give me X or I will do Y," would rather have X than do Y. Or else, he wouldn't be having the conversation.

Leading threat-assessment expert Gavin de Becker explains that threats more often represent desperation, not intention.[5] The threatener wants to influence events but has thus far failed to be effective. He, therefore, resorts to threats to induce anxiety in others, but "the threat means that at least for now (and usually forever), he favors words that alarm over actions that harm."[6] Returning to our scenario or any bluff, the less a person says, and the less he tries to sell you on his stance, the more legitimacy we give to the threat being carried out.

All the World Is a Show

To better understand the psychology at play in all this, it helps to think about how people handle themselves in general. A person who has high self-esteem isn't the one going around showing the world how great he is. It's the insecure person who puts on airs of superiority, drifting into arrogance and beyond, to compensate for how he really feels about himself. He is, in fact, trying to convey a "false self." Here, too, a person who lacks confidence in his ability to be effective—in his position—will attempt to compensate in order to portray the desired image. Overcompensation is a bluffer's glaring tell. He will constantly be restating his position in absolute terms. Confidence in one's position speaks for itself, just as a person's confidence in himself speaks for itself. It's the insecure person who has to tell us how confident he is—because that's the only way we're going to find out.

When people pretend to be confident, in a poker hand or in the real world, they manipulate how self-assured they appear. Because we equate confidence with calm, we will observe the person making an overt attempt to portray this image. For instance, law enforcement professionals know that a suspect may yawn as if to show he is relaxed, composed, or even bored. If the person is sitting, he may slouch or stretch his arms, covering more territory as if to demonstrate comfort and a feeling of ease. Or the suspect may busily pick lint off his slacks, trying to show he is preoccupied with something trivial and is clearly not worried about the charges. The only problem (for the guilty person) is that someone who is wrongly accused will be quite indignant, won't pay attention to such inconsequential activities, and won't try to promote the right image.

Poker Corner

In an attempt to manage how others perceive them, many amateur card players give themselves away with one or both of the following: First, when she gets a good hand, you'll be treated to "tsk, tsk" or a loud sigh accompanied by a shrug. She wants to let you know that she's glum and didn't get the cards she wanted, and she will provide you with a nice show of dismay and sadness—all fake. Second, when she has a weak hand, she'll stare at the flop (in Texas Hold'em) in a legitimate attempt to see whether she's missed something. However, with a strong hand, she will not only *not* stare at the flop, but she will gaze everywhere and anywhere around the room so that she can appear as uninterested as possible.

A bluff generally occurs in real time. But what do we do when we listen to an account of something that has already happened? Fortunately, deceitful narratives leave linguistic fingerprints, and in the next chapter you will learn how to tell whether the person's account of any conversation, interaction, or exchange is the whole truth and nothing but the truth or a complete work of fiction.

CHAPTER 8

Making Up Stories:
Alibis and Lullabies

Let's say you're interviewing a potential employee and she tells you a story about a previous employer. Is she making it up? You ask your teenager why he wasn't in school, and he offers up an alibi. Should you believe him or not? Some folks can spin mesmerizing tales, told with passion and rich in detail, except that they are complete and utter lies. To learn how to separate fact from fiction, we will begin with the details.

The Structure of a Statement and the Nature of Details

The inclusion or exclusion of details in either an oral or written statement is the source of much confusion when it comes to lie detection. Even among seasoned pros, some will tell you that any story with a lot of detail is most likely true, while others maintain that a truthful story or statement will contain only relevant facts, and anything else is an attempt to mislead. The confusion surrounding details is the result of several intertwining nuances that we can distill into three key factors:

Significance: How relevant the details are to the entirety of the story or the statement

Proportion and Placement: Where and how the details appear and, quantitatively speaking, how much time is devoted to them

Integration: How layered the details are and whether they are in proper physical and conversational context

Generally speaking, a high degree of relevant, vivid detail is a reliable indication of honesty. Deceitful statements, by contrast, are more likely to include a lot of irrelevant details or be unbalanced—meaning that the person may have mentioned only a few immaterial details, but they account for 50 percent of his entire statement or testimony. Finally, even when the above two criteria are met (details are both vivid and relevant), we must look at how and where they are integrated into the entire narrative.

To understand the nature of details, we need context, so let's pull back the lens to examine the structure of a statement. Common sense informs us that a truthful statement should be cohesive and coherent and not contain logical inconsistencies or contradictions, but this isn't always the case when it comes to traumatic events. The more intense the memory, the less we should expect a logical flow, with a beginning, middle, and end. Emotion guides our recall, and the most intense facets (barring dissociation) flood into the mind first. This is because adrenaline locks memories into place (which explains why we too easily remember insults or compliments—the fight-flight-freeze response engages, and the release of adrenaline intensifies the memory).[1]

The above notwithstanding, when a person is telling the truth, the lead-up to the "main event" or opening of the story is usually light on details, unless they are highly significant to the narrative. A deceitful story often contains a litany of irrelevant facts in the beginning because (a) the person is trying to establish himself as a trustworthy individual who is being as meticulous and specific as possible, and (b) there are many truthful elements to the story because it is during and after the "crime" or the lie when the details need to be rearranged and the truth altered, so it is relatively safe to engage in earnest recall of all of the particulars at the beginning without worrying about keeping the facts straight.

Someone making a deceitful statement often focuses heavily on irrelevant details to mimic the natural depth and richness found in a truthful statement. He peppers the conversation with minutiae to distract you from the truth, as if he's throwing sand in your face. This person knows that if his statement is too vague or too generic, you might not view it as trustworthy. At the same time, he also knows that the more complex the lie, the harder it is to maintain. He tends to, then, emphasize *truthful irrelevant information* in an attempt to duplicate the layers of truth, while simultaneously protecting himself from fabricating too many details that might come back to bite him later.

Keep in mind that unsolicited details—those that the person brings up without being prompted or asked—should be concise and in context, meaning they are immediately relevant to the point and not a tangential freight train. For example, stating that the mugger "reeked of cologne" is fine. An unnecessary extension becomes problematic and dubious: "He reeked of cologne. It was like the cheap stuff that probably sells for $5 a bottle. I don't know how people can wear that stuff." True? Perhaps. Relevant? No. We again draw a distinction between a traumatic and a nontraumatic event. The more immediate and serious the trauma, the more we expect these details to be concise and cogent. If, however, the person is just telling us a story about what happened—which, although dramatic, was not traumatic—then she might very well add "flavor" and "color" to the narrative. Again, though, the more emotionally charged the situation is—and the more pain the person experienced—the fewer unnecessary tangents we should expect to see.

Moving along, the main part of the narrative—where the action takes place—is often the most emotionally expressive and comprehensive in honest accountings, but it is quickly touched on or disproportionally truncated in deceitful ones. If the middle—the centerpiece of the discussion—is as short as the beginning and the end of the story, then deception is a possibility. Yet in and of itself, that is not a reliable indication. You always want to look for proportion and balance in a statement.

Finally, in much the same way that during a challenging conversation, interview, or interrogation a guilty person is happy to change the subject and end the conversation, a person writing out a false account is equally motivated to be finished. Therefore, deceitful accounts often lack a clearly defined retelling of the aftermath. Certainly, with emotionally charged and traumatic stories, we should see vivid layers of feelings and reflection, but for the liar this aspect is the most difficult to fabricate. He must construct not just what happened but also how it affected him and the range of emotions he would have genuinely felt at the time.

Compounding the challenge is that at the same time he must negate or accommodate an alternate reality—the truth. The introduction to his story allows him to stick closely to the facts, and the main part of the story needs a bit of tweaking, but the conclusion is cognitively draining and difficult for him to manufacture. This is especially so because he doesn't believe it is the crucial factor in honest accounts, so he ends it as quickly as he possibly can. Therefore, almost every made-up story will end with the climactic scene and a bare-minimum accounting of what transpired afterward.

Finally, be wary of narratives that end with statements such as "And that's all I can tell you," "I don't know what else to say," or "That's pretty much everything." Deception is indicated—though certainly not conclusively—when a person asserts, unsolicited, that he cannot tell you anything more. Think about it: If a person doesn't know anything else that could be helpful, then he won't say anything else. Yet because he *does* know something, he feels compelled to let you know he doesn't know anything more. This is a subtle but significant giveaway.

Clarifiers and Obvious Assertions

Any of the above factors are red flags, but a giant waving red flag is when someone qualifies the superfluous details himself and, more so, if he clarifies a detail that we can see is driven by a patently obvious motive. Consider the following statement:

"I woke up at, I think, 7:00 a.m. . . . no, maybe it was closer to 7:05 because I was really tired, and I needed to sleep a little bit more. Then I went downstairs to eat breakfast because I hadn't eaten much the night before, and so I was hungry. I made two—no, it was three, I remember now—eggs and two pieces of toast with butter."

This statement is not rich in relevant detail. Clarifying the exact time he got up and how many eggs he ate and then proceeding to explain the rationale behind these actions are a double whammy of signs of deceit. The reason the person adds narration is to supply you with reasonable motivations for his behavior, to explain that he is a thoughtful and logical person who acts rationally. He got up later *because* he was really tired. He ate breakfast *because* he hadn't eaten much the night before. He's a reasonable guy who does things that make sense, so there's no way he would ever do anything wrong!

Poker Corner

A player who throws his chips into the pot to place a bet and then makes an effort to stack the chips up neatly is perhaps bluffing. He doesn't want to trigger his opponent's calling reflex, which is in effect an emotional gag reflex. It means that he fears that lazily throwing in his chips will engage his opponent's ego, communicating the message: *I don't respect you enough to keep the pot neat.* This may sound like an overreaction, but it's the poker version of road rage. The slightest infraction is interpreted as a lack of respect, and a player can become enraged—impulsive, reckless, or aggressive—and call our bet even though he doesn't have a good hand (although it could still be better than the player's bluffing hand).

The psychology behind a person's willingness to question his own statement aloud is also instructive. He desperately wants to convince you that he is an honest, trustworthy individual. Therefore, he makes the effort to be perfectly accurate in his recollection of details. That way, you'll know that if he makes sure he tells you how many pieces of toast he ate, then he will be honest about everything else. Of course, if he is lying, then he can't be honest about everything else, so his level of precision and accuracy comes through on these irrelevant details. To be clear, if he qualifies *all* the details, relevant and inconsequential, that is not an indication of deceit—it indicates a (possibly neurotic) tendency for accuracy. This is often the case with people who love to talk and who are excited about sharing, connecting, and having conversations and also when a person is not defending himself against an allegation or does not in any way feel threatened by the interaction.

Someone making a deceitful statement often focuses heavily on irrelevant details to mimic the natural depth and richness found in a truthful statement. He peppers the conversation with minutiae to distract you from the truth, as if he's throwing sand in your face.

In short, a statement should contain relevant details, and any seemingly minor or insignificant ones should not take up the bulk of someone's presentation. The next step in determining the veracity of a statement is examining the *qualitative* nature of details. There are four key elements we need to analyze to help separate fact from fiction.

Vivid Narrative

Truthful statements are more likely to contain vivid descriptions of people's interactions and offer a verbatim re-creation or near-replication of any dialogue. A truthful account also provides a clear spatial representation—meaning where the person was, physically, in relation to other people and objects—as well as words that denote time and motion. For example, an accurate retelling of an exchange might sound like this:

> "John asked me, 'Why are you shaking? What's wrong with you?'"

> "I turned around and yelled at him, point-blank, 'Why are you following me?' and he just stared right back at me and didn't say a word."

Multiple Senses

The more layered the details are—in that they include more of one's senses, not just how something looked but also how it smelled, sounded, and felt—the more reliable they are. And when these details are embedded into the narrative, they are exceptionally reliable. For example, a multisense embedded interaction sounds like this:

> "The sun was in my eyes when I turned the corner, and that's when I ran smack into him."

"She knocked over her giant white mug, splashing me with scalding hot coffee."

Third-Party Perspective

We get another layer of authenticity when a detail contains the words or the perspective of another person. Suppose you ask your friend where she was last night. She tells you she had to work late. But you're not convinced that's true. So you press for more information and ask what she had for dinner. Here are two possible answers she might give:

> "Oh, I wasn't really hungry, so I just came home and watched some TV with my roommate. She made pasta, but I passed on it and then just went to bed."

> "Oh, I wasn't really hungry, so I just came home and watched some TV. My roommate was shocked that I would skip a meal, especially her famous pasta dish. She said, 'That's a first for you.'"

Both answers contain pretty much the same information, but the second adds another layer of depth—the roommate's point of view. Our instinct might tell us that this answer is more believable and more likely to be true than the first one. Certainly, not including another's point of view doesn't mean someone is lying, but the inclusion of it is a reliable indication of authenticity.

Scene Transitions and Negation

As long as we're talking about a nontraumatic event, a person who is telling the truth is recalling a memory, which is like a movie that's playing in his head. A person who is fabricating a story is forced to construct what happened, scene by scene, so it comes off more like a series of images or photographs strung together to create the impression of genuine movement.

If you recall what you did last night, you'd remember a sequence of events, where one scene flows into the next. If you constructed the details of what you did last night, it would sound less fluid. You would likely engage in what is called "scene chunking," where you state specific things that you did—"I got home . . . ate dinner . . . watched a little TV." But it is unlikely that you would offer any information about what happened between scenes, as you moved from one action to another. It's more telling when the details explain everything that happened but don't explain what did not.

Let's turn to the greatest fiction detective of all time to illustrate this psychological insight. The 1894 book *The Memoirs of Sherlock Holmes* by Sir Arthur Conan Doyle is a collection of short stories that includes "Silver Blaze," a mystery about the disappearance of a famous racehorse on the eve before a big race and the apparent murder of the horse's trainer.

Gregory [Scotland Yard detective]: "Is there any other point to which you would wish to draw my attention?"

Holmes: "To the curious incident of the dog in the night-time."

Gregory: "The dog did nothing in the night-time."

Holmes: "That was the curious incident."

Holmes solves the mystery when he realizes that the dog did not bark when one would expect it to do so. He concluded that the culprit was known to the dog, which is why it did not bark. The definitive clue was not what was present but rather what was absent. A person telling lies is talking about something that he didn't experience, so he focuses on getting his story straight. His thinking is notably one-dimensional, which is governed by the rule of primary thinking.

Negation is not a primary thought. If I said, "Don't think of an elephant," you would likely start thinking . . . about an elephant. That's because to process my request, you need to first think of what you shouldn't be thinking about—an elephant.[2] Sharing an experience you didn't have requires you to first imagine having the experience. This means that you'll think about what might have happened but not what might *not* have happened. The question is: How can we distinguish what didn't happen in a truthful story from what didn't happen in a fabricated story? Obviously, a near-infinite amount of details would not have occurred. The answer is that we take note of what I call *embedded bumps* (i.e., delays, difficulties, and disruptions) within the narrative because a made-up statement will likely *not* include these elements. For instance:

- "I knocked over my glass vase on the way back to the kitchen."
- "I burned my microwavable popcorn because I put the setting on too high."
- "It took him three or four tries for the engine to start."
- "He spilled half his coffee on himself, trying to get to the front."
- "Her hands were trembling so much she couldn't even open her purse."

These are examples of embedded bumps, which are difficult for someone to fabricate. If you didn't make popcorn or walk to the kitchen, the notion that you burned the popcorn or knocked over a vase (examples of negation) requires a deep level of thought. The notable exception is that we would expect to hear of bumps when someone uses them to keep the logic of a fictitious story intact (e.g., saying the car engine didn't start to explain a time delay or that you knocked over the vase to explain the glass on the floor).

The Ultimate Alibi Buster

Have you ever wanted to hook somebody up to a lie detector to see if he was telling you the truth? With the tactic that I first introduced in my book *Never Be Lied to Again*, you can instantly find out whether his story checks out or his alibi is nothing but a pack of lies—all by asking a few simple questions.[3]

Let's say a woman suspects that her boyfriend was not at the local movies with his brother, as he said, but went out on the town with a group of friends. Simply asking him whether he really did go to the movies would prompt him only to answer, "Yes." This is because if he was there, he would say, "Yes," and if he wasn't there, he would likely stick to his story and say, "Yes." Using the alibi-busting technique, she would ask two questions to confirm the facts and then introduce a made-up "fact." For instance, she would first ask, "What did you see?" and then perhaps, "Oh, what time did the movie let out?" Then she would introduce her own fact and say something like "Oh, I heard the traffic was all backed up at that hour because of a water main break." Now all she has to do is sit back and watch how he responds.

> As long as we're talking about a nontraumatic event, a person who is telling the truth is recalling a memory, which is like a movie that's playing in his head. A person who is fabricating a story is forced to construct what happened, scene by scene, so it comes off more like a series of images or photographs strung together to create the impression of genuine movement.

Her boyfriend is faced with an obvious problem. If he wasn't at the movies, he doesn't know whether to acknowledge that there was an accident because there might not have been one. And if he says there wasn't much traffic and there was, then she'll also know he wasn't really at the movies. Regardless of his answer, he will do the one thing that every liar does when confronted with this conundrum: He will hesitate while deciding how to answer. Remember, had he been at the theater he would have instantly said, "There was no traffic. What are you talking about?" But he isn't sure because he wasn't there, so he will hesitate in his answer and, in doing so, give himself away. On top of that, he will likely answer wrongly by agreeing with whatever she said because he doesn't know that she was making it up. Let's review:

- You start by asking two confirming questions and then introduce your own detail. Again, your detail has to be untrue. If the person merely confirms something that's actually true, you haven't learned anything new.
- Your detail must sound reasonable. Otherwise, the person you are questioning might think it's a joke.
- Your detail has to be something that would have directly affected the person, so he would have firsthand knowledge of this information.

If he pauses too long, changes the subject, or gives the wrong answer to your question, then you may not be getting the truth. Yet again, I have to encourage you not to rely on a single, isolated tactic. In this instance, it is possible that his hesitation means he is earnestly trying to recall the events of the evening.

This reminder notwithstanding, if someone's answer sounds pat and well rehearsed, there's a fair chance she was expecting the question and took the time to get her story straight. Having facts and details at her fingertips that she should not easily recall is a good indication that she has prepared. For instance, consider a person who when asked where she was on a particular day two months ago responds, "I went to work, left at five-thirty, had dinner at the Eastside Diner until seven forty-five, and then went straight home." Or suppose a police detective questions a suspect. If the person is able to recall what he did and where he was on a given date two years earlier, something is very wrong. Most of us can't remember what we had for breakfast yesterday morning.

It's one thing to be tight-lipped or to tell a white lie; it's quite another to proactively seek to use another individual for one's personal gain. We all know smooth talkers and manipulative rogues; and then there are real con artists. The good news is that their strategies are highly predictable, and once you know their playbook, you can easily foresee and counter their next moves. In the next chapter, you'll learn how to turn the tables and never be taken advantage of again.

CHAPTER 9

Tricks of the Trade

Con artists are masters of misdirection, which happens to be the central element of magic.[1] And like any good magician, a con artist not only moves our attention to where they want it but often pairs their sleight of hand with an engaging story. They know that fanciful storytelling is more persuasive than boldface lies.

Nobel Prize laureate Daniel Kahneman explains that people have two modes of thought: System 1, which comes naturally, is automatic and intuitive and therefore fast and often emotional; and System 2, which is more analytical and logical and thus slower, requires conscious thought and mental energy.[2] A story automatically activates System 1, which means that we tend to accept it at face value. The task of the con artist is to keep us from switching to System 2, where we can rationally process what is happening. Depending on the dynamics of the situation, he will employ a number of psychological tactics that take advantage not only of our good nature but also of human nature itself.

Manipulation in Progress

Let's take a look at a con artist's process through the *imposter* scam, which is the most common form of fraud in the United States. To gain compliance quickly and unquestionably—to sell their story—the con artist seeks to make the subject more susceptible. Their method typically follows this pattern:

Establish authority $\rightarrow$ Stun $\rightarrow$ Reinforce credibility $\rightarrow$ Tell a story

1. ***Establish authority:*** A story is only as credible as the person who tells it, which is why a con artist will often claim to be a trusted source and person in authority (e.g., government agent, lottery official). As children, we are rightly taught that obedience to authority is proper and necessary. As adults, we are often all too intimidated by those in authority and confer on them traits that are unearned, such as intelligence, compassion, and goodness. We automatically believe, therefore, that they have our best interests at heart. We rely on their expertise to serve our interests and do not easily question their commands and decisions. However, we may tend to obey authority figures even when deference flies in the face of reason and common sense.

   Leading social psychologist Dr. Robert Cialdini explains that symbols of authority—titles, clothes, and trappings—influence our behavior and lead to mechanical obedience. He cites one such experiment involving a "doctor" prescribing an unusually high and dangerous dose of medication over the phone that resulted in a 95 percent compliance rate. The nurses disregarded hospital policy (which forbade orders from doctors by phone) and their own judgment (that the dose was clearly unsafe). The researchers concluded that the intelligence of the nurses following the orders was "nonfunctioning."[3]

2. **Stun:** When we are distracted or under pressure, we will tend to believe even highly dubious statements.[4] Alleging that you are in trouble with the law, excitedly proclaiming you the winner of a substantial prize, or offering you a once-in-a-lifetime opportunity, a con artist tries to paralyze your thought process with overwhelming fear or excitement. This is because strong emotions practically shut down the prefrontal cortex—the logic center of the brain. Adrenaline hijacks the brain and redirects control from the prefrontal cortex ("the thinking brain") to the amygdala ("the fear and anxiety response center"). We can then no longer think clearly and make rational decisions.

3. **Reinforce credibility:** Before you have a chance to question their authenticity, the scammer rattles off information about you that they already know to be true. When we hear at least two truisms, we are prone to accept at face value what follows.[5] It might go something like this:

"This is Agent Smith at the IRS. Is this Mr. Brown?

"Yes."

"You reside at 123 River Lane and you recently traveled abroad. Is that correct?"

"Yes."

"Mr. Brown, you're in an awful lot of trouble . . ." Or "Have I got some great news for you!"

If this conversation was in person, official-looking documents would no doubt be at hand. It never ceases to amaze me just how easily swayed we become by printed material. Just because someone hands you a business card or points

to a color graph as proof doesn't make everything or anything that he's saying true.

4. ***Tell a story:*** Now they spin a tale, all the while reinforcing
their authority and the consequences of noncompliance.
Their logic always follows the same route: If you do as they
say, they can make your troubles go away (or deliver on the
promised riches).

Be especially alert if they press you to make a quick
decision and keep you focused on a narrow set of "facts."
Context is king. Don't get lost in the story. Take the
time to evaluate the information, which will slow down
your lightning-fast brain and engage your slower-thinking
System 2.

The Connection Deception

The seasoned swindler may set the table for compliance long before he
ever tells you his story. To do this, he will seek to deepen an emotional
bond with you by building greater trust and confidence. The *con* in *con
artist* is, after all, short for *confidence.* Courtesy of human nature, we tend
to trust, and subsequently be influenced by, people who are like us and
who like us.

You're Like Me, and You Like Me

It is not true that opposites attract. We actually prefer people who are
similar to us and who have similar interests.[6] We may find someone
interesting because of how different he is from us, but it's the similarities and commonalities that generate mutual liking. Like attracts like.

Akin to this law is the principle of "comrades in arms." People who
go through life-changing situations together tend to create a significant
bond. For instance, soldiers who fight battles or fraternity pledges who
get hazed together usually develop strong friendships. This is also a

powerful bonding method even if the experience was not shared but similarly experienced. As a result, two people who have never met but who have shared a similar previous experience—whether it's an illness or winning the lottery—can become instant friends. It is the "she understands me" mentality that generates these warm feelings for each other. In initial interactions, be aware when you're asked about your hobbies, hometown, values, favorite foods, and so forth, only to be followed with the shocking revelation: "Me, too. What a coincidence!" Or when a person initiates a revelation (e.g., "Nice watch. I have an identical one"; "That's a beautiful dog. It reminds me of the one I had growing up"; "You look like you're having a day like mine.").

The expression "flattery will get you nowhere" couldn't be further from the truth. It will get you many places that you would have otherwise never gone. One study showed that most of us are so thirsty for praise that we report greater liking for a stranger when we receive a compliment, even when we are aware that the flatterer has a clear ulterior motive.[7] Does this mean that you should be wary of every compliment and assume a malevolent agenda? Of course not. But you do need to be mindful that flattery interferes with your assessment and judgment.

We are all susceptible to falling for a con to some degree, but when our natural immunity is compromised, we become all the more receptive. In *The Confidence Game*, author Maria Konnikova writes:

> When it comes to predicting who will fall [victim to a con artist], personality generalities tend to go out the window. Instead, one of the factors that emerges is circumstance: it's not who you are, but where you happen to be at this particular moment in your life.[8]

She explains that when our emotional resilience is frayed, our cognitive defenses of reason and judgment are down, and we become particularly vulnerable. When we are lonely, financially downtrodden, or dealing with a serious injury, trauma, or major life change, we're most at risk.[9]

In other words, we can't underestimate the strength of the psychological pull. For instance, when we are in crisis, we often look for someone to talk to, to share with. Our number one emotional need is to feel connected to others. Pain—emotional or physical—causes us to feel alone, and loneliness further exacerbates the pain. When we establish a connection with another person, we no longer feel alone and the intensity of our pain is eased. Desperate for relief, we become all too willing to dispense with reason. We blind ourselves to the truth because we so eagerly want to believe.

Even as the logic of our decision becomes murky and the facts no longer add up, the ego forces us forward. Clinging tightly to an ever-fading hope, we do the job of the con artist for him. We sell ourselves. He no longer needs to exert pressure when our own fear of ("yet another") failure fuels our willingness to believe him.

Outside of the con, why do rational people sometimes make irrational decisions? Why do we willingly throw good money after bad? As any master stock trader will advise, we start losing money the second we allow our emotions to influence our trading decisions. When investors put on blinders, ignore empirical evidence, and dedicate themselves to recovering as much of their loss as possible, we say they're "chasing a loss." Our allegiance to stubborn persistence tends to become stronger once we have invested time, money, or energy into something—whether it's a tumbling stock, doomed relationship, or dead-end job. It's easy to succumb to the sunk-cost fallacy: *I can't quit now because I'll lose everything I've already invested!* Misguided commitment is nothing more than a delay tactic, which is the toxic offspring of denial—a refusal to accept that we have to make a change.

The Bonds That Lie

Back to the con. Whether you've been chatting with him for five minutes or have known him for five months, you think to yourself, *This is someone who really gets me.* But when the emotional tether is not as strong as the con artist needs (for whatever he wants from you), he will weave in the strongest strand of compliance: trust.

The difference between faith and trust is profound. For example, we can have faith that things will work out, or that a friend will come through for us, but we may still be plagued by worry and moments of doubt. When we have trust, however, negative thoughts do not fill our mind. We do not dwell on or worry about the outcome. Trust is an intellectual process, a natural outgrowth of an unblemished record. This is why he must establish trust. The time will come when he asks you to do something that makes little or no sense. If you trust him, then you will act quickly, without question or hesitation. Here is how he creates that trust.

> Courtesy of human nature, we tend to trust, and subsequently be influenced by, people who are like us and who like us.

The Trust Accelerator

When a person shares private aspects of her life, this invokes two psychological influences. First, sharing creates unearned trust. When someone opens up, you think, *If she trusts me, then I should be able to trust her.* We needn't assume a malevolent intention. She might be emotionally fragile and need to unburden herself, seeking only a listening ear. That said, premature revelations, disclosures, or secrets, in combination with the other tactics, may be an attempt to force a connection—giving them psychological momentum, that they have somehow earned your trust.

This activates the second influence: You will be moved to reciprocate because it's only fair. When someone gives you something, like time, information, or a gift, you'll often feel indebted. Most salespeople are aware that if they invest a lot of time with you—showing you a product, demonstrating how it works—you will feel more obligated to buy it, even if you're not sure you really want it. Here, too, when a person shares herself with us, we may feel uneasy unless we reciprocate and share of ourselves.

Cialdini explains the unethical approach of a top-producing salesperson who sold expensive heat-activated fire alarm systems. His in-home pitch started with a short test on fire knowledge. While the homeowners were busy jotting down their answers, he would invariably say that he had "forgotten some really important information" in the car that he needed to get. "I don't want to interrupt the test," he would add, "so would you mind if I let myself out and back into your home?" Cialdini notes that "the answer was always some form of 'Sure, go ahead.' Oftentimes it required giving him a door key."[10] Allowing someone to enter your home, on his own, is a tacit sign of trust: *I trust him because I let him enter my house by himself. He must be trustworthy because the only alternative is that I'm a complete fool.* The act itself subconsciously embeds the belief that the salesman is someone who is trustworthy; and we listen to people we trust.

> When a person shares private aspects of her life, this invokes two psychological influences. First, sharing creates unearned trust. . . . [Then] you will be moved to reciprocate because it's only fair.

In parts I and II, we learned ways to read people in specific situations. Knowing the kind of person we're dealing with will assist us in predicting their behavior and guiding it when necessary. In part III, you will discover how to assess a person's nature and how to detect the warning signs of a dominant and controlling personality. You'll also learn how to identify the potential for, and trajectory of, pathology—in other words, how emotional illness will manifest itself if their psyche is beginning to show cracks. Are they likely to become predator or prey?

PART III

TAKING A PSYCHOLOGICAL SNAPSHOT

Pierce anyone's public persona to access their internal operating system and you'll know what makes them tick—what drives them forward and what holds them back. Find out their deepest values and core beliefs that shape their desires, fears, and insecurities. Understand people better than they know themselves, and in the process gain a greater awareness of yourself.

CHAPTER 10

A Peek into Personality and Mental Health

Even though *personality type* isn't a clinical or scientific term, most people understand the concept to mean *how someone generally behaves* or to refer to their *temperament*. Are they usually relaxed or high-strung? Do they like to be in control or let others take the lead? Do they tend to see the proverbial glass as half-empty or half-full? The pioneering linguist and clinical psychiatrist Walter Weintraub explains that what we call "personality" is a construct of observable ways of dealing with internal and external stress.[1]

These traits, then, get heightened and more obvious when someone is experiencing some degree of stress. In that moment, their defense mechanisms engage, and their language patterns become immediately discernible. In broad strokes, a more dominant personality tends to redirect fear and anxiety away from himself, while a submissive person often internalizes it, absorbing it. For example, a person can choose to express his exasperation to a situation in a few ways, such as:

STATEMENT A: "I can't open the window."
STATEMENT B: "The window is stuck."
STATEMENT C: "The window is broken."

Each of these asserts the same reality from a different outlook, with phrasing that reveals how the speaker sees himself and frames his world. The first statement, "I can't open the window," is classically self-focused and is likely spoken by the more submissive personality. The second statement, "The window is stuck," is outwardly focused and representative of a dominant personality. Neither of these responses indicates better or worse emotional health (in general) or feelings of anxiety (within the situation). It only reveals whether the person is prone to assuming or shifting responsibility. Once again, we remind ourselves that we want to observe a pattern of syntax rather than one-off statements before making a determination of one's personality.

The third statement, however, is more instructive than the other two. Here, the individual concludes that her inability to open the window is not due to her inefficiency or that the window is in a temporary state of "being stuck," but rather (a) it is to blame, and (b) its state is permanent and absolute. Later in the book, we will discuss why labeling the window in such terms—broken rather than stuck—casts a question mark on the person's emotional well-being; and when it's spiced up with adjectival and adverbial intensifiers (e.g., "The damn window is totally busted"), we might want to hit the pathological alarm bell if the pattern is typical and persists.

A more dominant personality tends to redirect fear and anxiety away from himself, while a submissive person often internalizes it, absorbing it.

Likewise, the third response becomes more concerning should her helplessness turn into total resignation. In other words, the broader implication of the window being in an irreparable state of "brokenness" is that she perceives herself to be permanently incapable and would sound something like "I just can't open the window" or "I can never open windows."

The Trajectory of Mental Illness

Although neither Statement A nor Statement B can be said to reflect more robust mental health than the other, they *do* hint at the potential path of mental *unwellness*—a disorder—should it develop.

Psychological disorders are commonly classified as either *ego-dystonic* or *ego-syntonic*. Behaviors, thoughts, or feelings that upset a person and make them uncomfortable are ego-dystonic. The person doesn't like them and doesn't want them, and that combination makes a person more inclined to seek treatment. Ego-dystonic issues are often mood disorders (also called *affective disorders*), a classification that includes depression, bipolar disorder, and anxiety disorder. Each of these disorders has sub-types with a range of signs and symptoms, depending on the person and the severity of the case. Sufferers are inclined toward negative thoughts, rumination, and self-focus (and, in some personality types, hostility and impulsivity). They are often hypersensitive to everyday stressors, become easily frustrated and overwhelmed, and are emotionally reactive, which makes it difficult for them to think clearly and cope with stress. Mood or affective disorders tend to develop from the submissive personality.

Personality disorders, on the other hand, are ego-syntonic and are compatible with a person's self-image and worldview. These include borderline personality disorder, antisocial personality disorder, and nar-cissistic personality disorder. From this person's standpoint, their thoughts, behavior, and feelings are all parts of their identity.[2] Even if everyone else believes that they are suffering from a disorder, they refuse to look inward and will assume that everyone else has the problem, not them. As you might guess from what we've covered, people with per-sonality disorders tend to have dominant personalities.

Just to recap, the following flowchart shows the decay of mental health with the statistically likely, although far from certain, traits:

submissive (e.g., compliant, codependent) → affective disorder (e.g., anxiety, depression) dominant (e.g., hostile, aggressive, suspicious, cruel, manipulative) $\rightarrow$ personality disorder (e.g., narcissism, antisocial tendencies)

The Matrix of Mood and Status

When I introduced the accident-prone cadet in chapter 4, it was to show that whenever people interact inconsistently with their status, we gain an insight into more than their relationship; we have a picture of their personality and mental condition. Incorporating a person's mood into the equation focuses our assessment even more sharply.

Mood is the shadow of self-esteem, temporarily lifting or deflating us, coloring how we see our world and ourselves.[3] A person who acts and interacts in a way that clinicians would call "mood congruent"—consistent with their mood—reveals little. When you're in a good mood—brimming with feelings (fleeting though they may be) of confidence and control—you generally treat the people around you with greater kindness and respect. In the moment, you feel "complete." You can shift your awareness outward to the world around you.

As our mood sours, we are prone to become emotionally stingy and less accommodating to others. We may show kindness or give respect to those we need rather than those who are in need. In such a state, our frustration level naturally increases and our tolerance decreases. The ease with which we rise above our own pain, emotional or physical, and shift attention to the welfare of another is a reliable marker of emotional health—even more so, when we do so with patience and compassion.

What happens when you add status back into the equation? A person of higher status who is in a negative state but who manages to put his own concerns aside in favor of the other's needs—even when he doesn't "need to"—demonstrates the apex of emotional health. This magnanimity might range from speaking politely and smiling (mild behaviors) to an outright expression of empathy. If this person with higher status (who is in a bad mood) acts with a blunt or gruff demeanor, that's actually not as instructive or revealing. Why? Because this is what's called both "mood and status congruent." Although it does not indicate exemplar emotional health, it does fall inside the spectrum of "normal."

Likewise, we should expect a person of high status and in a positive state to maintain a polite and cordial demeanor; again, such behavior is not revealing. However, an unpleasant attitude and rude behavior signals a hostile personality, and speaking harshly or acting aggressively exemplifies emotional instability. In fact, the recipe for a royal pain is bad mood + low self-esteem + high status. You will witness extreme irritation and, depending on their personality, either passive or active anger. This is particularly so if their status is only temporarily conferred (i.e., customer) and they have no other outlet for their bubbling frustrations. A fleeting opportunity to exert their power is often too much for them to let pass.

The higher our self-esteem, the more we are driven to behave responsibly, regardless of our mood. But as self-esteem sinks, the ego rises, and our mood holds greater sway over our behavior. Think small children having wild mood swings—sudden tantrums, erupting in mindless exuberance. Adults who act and react based on their state, how they feel in the moment, tend to have lower self-esteem. The extent that mood overrides lower status and is unable to be kept in check—and the magnitude of the breach—is telling of one's emotional health. Punching out a commanding officer or cursing out one's boss is of greater magnitude than skipping a "please" or "thank-you" in conversation with them.

Low status and a positive state should ensure a polite and cordial demeanor—again because it is mood and status congruent. Rude behavior under these conditions indicates an overly aggressive, dominant personality. The deviation from both mood and status suggests an actual trait and cements our personality and pathology snapshot.

Certainly, a person's speech could just reflect his mood or exasperation within the situation. Emotional distress, not unlike acute physical pain, naturally directs our focus inward. Our language, then, may be blunt and seemingly ungracious. Again, the logic is clear: A person drowning will shout "Help!" or "Help me!" and not "I'm sorry to trouble you, kind folks, but if you wouldn't mind, I would appreciate it if you could throw me a rope." This person's interactions and correspondence may give the impression of power or perceived status when, in actuality, they feel completely helpless and vulnerable.

Yet again, that's why it's important to look for patterns of behavior and not just isolated incidents. Remember: Frequency, duration, intensity, and context determine whether you are observing a state or a trait.

High Status, Negative Mood	**High Status, Positive Mood**
Impolite and blunt demeanor, not instructive. Pleasant and empathetic behavior demonstrates solid emotional health.	Polite and pleasant behavior, not instructive. Unpleasant or rude demeanor signals a hostile personality and emotional instability.
Low Status, Negative Mood	**Low Status, Positive Mood**
Polite and poised behavior indicates emotional solvency. Impolite or blunt demeanor indicates a mild breach in emotional health, with rude or aggressive behavior signaling greater emotional instability.	Polite and pleasant behavior, not instructive. Unpleasant or rude demeanor signals a hostile personality and emotional disturbance.

Decoding Someone's Core Nature

Linguistic giveaways about personality also exist on a granular level, through subtle language cues and passing encounters. Higher and lower status dynamics are relevant wherever we have a fixed hierarchy of power (e.g., manager/employee, captain/private, teacher/student). Outside of these situations, context matters because status can be in flux. In other words, status is conferred on whoever is the "boss" within any specific situation. A seller with a hot-ticket item and many interested buyers holds leverage and therefore, in this situation, has higher status, even if in other contexts she doesn't have power. Conversely, a commissioned salesclerk in a clothing store "needs" the buyer and is thus of lower status. What's important about adding context to the mix is that it's precisely when status is temporarily conferred or altogether neutralized that one's nature—either dominant or submissive—emerges unobstructed. Understanding context allows you to build a psychological profile more quickly and will help you predict the trajectory of mental illness should it develop in the person you're watching.

Connectors versus Confronters

I once had a memorable conversation with my barber, who told me that sometimes customers will absentmindedly leave without paying. Calling out "You didn't pay" or "You forgot to pay" was too uncomfortable for him, so he just let them walk out the door. I encouraged him to rephrase this as "Did you want to pay next time?" He has done so ever since, with complete ease. Let's take a look at why.

"What did you say?" asks one person. "What was it you were saying?" asks another. Both seek the same information, but the first person's question has a more demanding, commanding tone. The mother who tells her child, "We will be getting ready for bed in five minutes," sounds gentler than the one who says, "Get ready for bed in five minutes." The teacher who asks, "What did you think was the right answer?" sounds less threatening than the one who inquires, "What's the answer?" This shifting of verb tense signals the speaker's desire to connect rather than confront and goes to the core of someone's nature and relationship status. Qualifiers also do the same job quite nicely (e.g., "We should be getting ready for bed"; "I think you may have forgotten to settle the tab").

A general rule is that a more agreeable person uses language that builds connection and avoids confrontation. Their less agreeable counterpart uses language that is more controlling and uninhibited by confrontation.[4] In the unhealthy extreme, the former avoids confrontation at all costs, which may include repressing their true feelings and desires, while the latter welcomes and even fosters opportunities for strife and conflict.

For example, you walk into a convenience store and ask the cashier where the newspapers are. They may respond with a range of answers, such as:

RESPONSE A: "Over there." (incomplete and direct)

RESPONSE B: "They're over there." (complete and direct)

RESPONSE C: "They should be right over there." (qualifier)

RESPONSE D: "You'll find them right over there." (future tense)

RESPONSE E: "I think you may find them right over there."
(double qualifier and future tense)

All the responses answer the question, but the subtext of each reveals something about the responder. Responses A and B show the typical language pattern of a more dominant personality, and Responses C, D, and E of a more agreeable (and potentially submissive) personality.

Now let's filter through the two main factors: status and mood. The maître d' of an upscale restaurant may be more deferential than the cashier at a convenience store because of the shift in status, and thus Responses D and E do not give us an indication of their personality—because it is consistent with the status dynamic. On the flip side, Responses A and B do give us a glimpse of their personality because they deviate from the supposed dynamic. Let's take another example.

Ringing up a purchase in the store, the salesclerk says:

STATEMENT A: "You owe one hundred seventy-eight dollars."
STATEMENT B: "That will be one hundred seventy-eight dollars."

After you make a purchase in the store, the salesclerk hands you the receipt and says either:

STATEMENT A: "There" or "Here," or they say nothing.
STATEMENT B: "This will be yours" or "Here we are."

Once again, in a high-end store, we would expect Statements B instead of Statements A. But when status is neutralized, we more readily see the individual's personality coming through. A convenience store clerk who uses Statement B language likely has a more agreeable nature, while Statement A language yields no insight within the same context. However, a salesperson in a high-end store who uses Statement A language is either having a bad day, which means it speaks to their state, or has a more dominant personality. If their mood is unknown, then we have to observe their behavior to see whether a pattern emerges that can move our assessment from (temporary) state to (permanent) trait.

In response to a question on hours of operation, which answer signals a more easygoing and pleasant receptionist?

RESPONSE A: "We're closed on Sunday."
RESPONSE B: "I believe we're closed this Sunday."

Accepting that the receptionist is fully aware that the office is closed, "I believe" qualifies their answer to cushion the impact for the questioner. In chapter 5, I explained that the use of a qualifier signals anxiety or insecurity only when expressing subjective, and not objective, information. Let's modify the second response to show an even stronger contrast:

RESPONSE A: "We're closed on Sunday."

RESPONSE C: "I'm sorry, I believe we're going to be closed this Sunday."

When a person of equal or higher status uses softer language, it is because they are tuned into the needs of the other, which indicates empathy and corresponding emotional health. They do not need to assert their authority to compensate for their own insecurities. For instance, a manager fires an employee with one of the following statements:

STATEMENT A: "You're fired."

STATEMENT B: "I'm sorry, but we're going to have to let you go."

It is clear that Statement A makes no attempt to sugarcoat the firing. In the second phrasing, the manager uses *we* instead of *I* to diffuse responsibility; starting with *I* rather than *you* points to inward orientation. Offering an apology and using future tense further reduces the impact.

Another example: If you're attempting to enter an unauthorized area without proper clearance, which security guard has the more amiable nature (and is possibly easier to sway if they seek to avoid conflict)?

GUARD A: "Stop, you can't go in there. What are you doing?"

GUARD B: "Excuse me, I can't let you go in there."

Guard A issues a command, uses the second-person *you,* and then asks a rhetorical question as an anger signal. Guard B uses *I*-language, negative language (signaling possible anxiety), and offers up an apology.[5] The delineation between the two psyches is striking when you know what to listen for.

The Nature of Words

Some linguistic giveaways are intuitive. Agreeable people use more positive emotion words (e.g., *happy, inspiring, wonderful*) and fewer negative ones (e.g., *hate, destroy, annoyed, angry*).[6] They write and talk more about home, family, and communication, and they avoid dark or sensitive topics and language (e.g., words such as *coffins, torture, death*).[7]

In stark contrast, their less agreeable counterparts use negative language and words related to anger (e.g., "I hate . . ."; "I'm sick and tired of . . ."; "I can't stand . . .").[8] Research findings show that more agreeable people swear less. In Facebook status updates, for instance, the five words that best identify individuals who rank low in agreeableness are all swear words.[9] And the word *thank-you* in Facebook status updates is most correlated to the trait of agreeableness.[10] A healthy perspective allows us to focus on the positive and helps us foster an attitude of appreciation and gratitude.[11] This psychological insight is captured beautifully by the pen of the poet C. S. Lewis: "Praise almost seems to be inner health made audible."[12]

Let's unpack the psychology. Without perspective, all of the good in our lives remains out of focus. An egocentric person—one who lacks perspective—is interested only in what they lack, what is owed, where life has come up short. And where there is no gratitude, there is no joy.[13] If we think about the people we know who have a sense of gratitude, these same individuals are the most joyful. By contrast, those who lack appreciation for what they have live in a cycle of unrealized expectations, frustration, and anger. They are filled with anger and resentment not because of anything major, but because their entire focus is on trivial matters that consume them with negativity.

wide perspective (i.e., higher self-esteem, smaller ego) → greater context → more meaning → humility stirs → gratitude surges → joy flows → emotional stability narrow perspective (i.e., lower self-esteem, bigger ego) $\rightarrow$ diminished context $\rightarrow$ less meaning $\rightarrow$ arrogance grows $\rightarrow$ fuels anger, resentment, and frustration $\rightarrow$ emotional instability

Mindset and Metaphors

A metaphor creates a bridge between the new and the known. It packs a punch, metaphorically speaking, of course, because it conveys information compactly and precisely. The imagery and representations that we use announce our mindset.

A sales manager, for example, may have a penchant for describing the optimal workplace with a combative metaphor (e.g., "We're like a Delta Force team"). Given the presence of collaborative evidence, we might infer that to him, everything is a contest in which there can be only one winner. You're either a hammer or a nail, a winner or a loser, and life is a zero-sum equation. One person's gain is equivalent to another's loss.

Even in a cooperative environment, the more dominant personality will tend toward language that confirms their outlook, with statements reminiscent of "We crushed them," "We were unstoppable," and "They didn't know what hit them," and, even more *I*-centered and unhealthy, "I was on fire. I was not going to walk away a loser. They're the losers, not me." This is quite different from, "We pulled together, worked hard, and gave it our all" or "The other team really brought out our best." To the keen observer, the small leaks are geysers.

Ask a first-grade teacher how they envision their role, and we would expect to hear a gentle, nurturing response (e.g., "to ensure that each beautiful flower has the right amount of sunlight and water to blossom" or, perhaps less saccharine, "to inspire a love of learning"). I recall a teacher complaining to me that the principal would not give him more latitude to discipline the class as he saw fit. "I could squeeze so much more out of them," he would say. "They just need a push to excel."

Remember, he was talking about five- and six-year-olds! The objective was not troubling, but his language was. Rephrased, the same sentiments become reasonable: "I want to help them maximize their potential," "There's so much greatness inside of them," or "I just want them to shine." Using words such as *squeezing* and *pushing* reflects not only a mindset but perhaps a distorted view of education as well.

In the next chapter, you will learn how to delve more deeply into your assessment and get to a person's fundamental story of "I." In doing so, you will begin to assess their insecurities and areas of resistance. This is not to take advantage of anybody but to better understand them— so you can help them and also protect yourself. Once you become aware of a person's triggers, you can predict when they will lash out, feel the need to assert themselves, and seek to usurp control. Equally helpful is learning more about ourselves and our own triggers. With greater self-awareness, you can enhance the quality of your life and your relationships.

CHAPTER 11

Narrative Identity:
Reading Hearts and Souls

Imagine you're chaperoning a school trip for twenty-five children. After the kids get off the bus, you dutifully take a head count in the lobby of the aquarium. You count twenty-four. Yikes. You count again. Twenty-five. Hooray. You then march the kids in to explore the wonders of the sea. What's the problem? Why did you assume that twenty-four was incorrect but twenty-five was correct? Only because you have twenty-five students. So when you counted the number that confirmed this, you stopped. But there is no reason to assume that it is any less likely that you counted one child twice (arriving at the correct number) than that you forgot to count one child the first time around.

People tend to find whatever they're looking for and see what they expect to see. Always on the lookout for corroborating evidence that proves us right, we turn a blind eye to any evidence that doesn't conform to our expectations. This is a phenomenon known as *confirmation bias*. We home in on what confirms our thinking, and we subconsciously filter out inconsistencies.

When confirmation bias is at work, the evidence arranges itself— almost mystically—into ready-labeled patterns. This is part of the neurobiological process the brain uses to make sense of the world. Our brains basically make files, just as we do on our computers. In our brains, this categorization falls under the umbrella of mental shortcuts, called *heuristics*. These shortcuts allow us to process the world without making independent decisions every time we choose. Imagine if we had to solve every single problem from scratch, from how to operate the coffee maker to how to get to work. We'd never get anything done. Mental shortcuts save the day.

Jumping to Conclusions

Heuristics are useful for helping us solve problems efficiently, but they can lead to biases that cause us to slip into a "guilty until proven innocent" mode. For example, if a detective investigating a woman's murder knows that a high percentage of murdered women are killed by their spouses, they might be more likely to assume that the spouse did it and begin to mentally filter evidence to fit their theory. This is not to say that statistics aren't a useful tool; the challenge lies in giving them proportional, rather than exclusive, weight. If a doctor frequently treats people with depression, they might hear a patient's complaint of symptoms such as fatigue, energy loss, weight gain, and decreased libido and leap to one particular conclusion. (*Aha! Depression!*) But the problem could also be hypothyroidism or fifty other maladies with similar symptoms. As the saying goes, "To a hammer, everything looks like a nail."

We also tend to fall back on the representativeness heuristic—whereby we group people into categories based on their similarities to a typical member of the group. Once you're labeled, it's assumed that you share all the features of other members in your category, and they share yours. If we have a preconceived notion about a particular group, we may jump to conclusions about individual members of that group, even stubbornly ignoring evidence that refutes our conclusions. In the words of William James: "A great many people think they are thinking when they are merely rearranging their prejudices."

Biases create expectations; not unlike our brain creating file folders to chunk information together, we develop schemas or blueprints that help us anticipate what we'll find when we encounter a particular concept, category, person, or situation. Schemas help us fill in the blanks quickly. Unfortunately, they can nudge us to fill in some of those blanks with wrong answers. If we approach new information with a preconceived notion that it should fit into our grand schema, we may keep information that conforms to our expectations and discard information that doesn't.

> Bringing awareness to our biases helps neutralize their impact and enhances our ability to evaluate another person or situation objectively.

Bringing awareness to our biases helps neutralize their impact and enhances our ability to evaluate another person or situation objectively. If we enter a conversation, negotiation, or personal relationship believing that we know everything already, then our ego will deftly confirm all that we believe to be true. Only the exceptional person is willing to look at what they don't want to see, listen to what they don't want to hear, and believe that which they wish did not exist.

But this is only half the story. It is an elegant irony that once we diffuse the heuristic impact that interferes with our assessment, we can more effectively build a profile, in large part *because* of heuristics.

The Director's Cut

We are aware that people tend to find whatever they're looking for and see what they expect to see. Our assessment crystallizes when we ask, "Why does a person need to see that which they are looking for in the first place?" People see themselves, others, and their world in the way they need to in order to reconcile what they are seeing with their personal narrative—to make sense of themselves, their choices, and their lives.[1] This leads to what psychologist Daniel Kahneman terms *associative coherence*—the notion that "everything reinforces everything else." He writes:

Our chronic discomfort with ambiguity leads us to predictable, comfortable, familiar interpretations, even if they are only partial representations of or fully disconnected from reality. . . . Other things that don't fit fall away by the wayside. We're enforcing coherent interpretations. We see the world as much more coherent than it is.[2]

The greater our ego, the more vulnerable we feel and the greater our drive to predict and control our world. Coherence, not facts, feeds the belief that the world is predictable and known. We then seek out, see, and interpret the world to fit our narrative rather than adjusting our worldview to fit reality. Essentially, we color the world so that we are untainted.

Sanity is synonymous with *perspective.* The clearer our perspective, the more reality we allow in and the more objective and rational are our attitudes, thoughts, and behaviors. When we refuse to responsibly acknowledge any aspect of ourselves or our lives, the ego engages to "protect" us, and it shifts the blame elsewhere. In other words, we think, *If there is nothing wrong with me, then there must be something wrong with you.* For us to remain unblemished in our own minds, we are forced to distort the world around us, and if our grasp on reality is flawed, then our adjustment to life will suffer. Emotional instability is fundamentally a lack of clarity in the degree to which the ego colors our ability to see ourselves and the world as it is. When a person loses his sanity—the ability to see, accept, and respond to his world—it means that he has lost all perspective.

Mirror, Mirror on the Wall

Ralph Waldo Emerson writes, "People do not seem to realize that their opinion of the world is also a confession of character." This is not just a clever quip but a piercing insight into human nature. People look at the world as a reflection of themselves.[3] If they see the world as a corrupt place, they feel on some level—unconsciously, probably—that they are corrupt. If they see honest working people, that is frequently how they see themselves. That's why the con artist is the first one to accuse another of cheating.

The old saying "What Susie says about Sally says more of Susie than of Sally" turns out to have a strong psychological basis. Research finds that when you ask someone to rate the personality of another person— a close colleague, an acquaintance, or a friend—their response gains you direct insight into their personality traits and their own emotional health. Indeed, findings show "a huge suite of negative personality traits are associated with viewing others negatively."[4] Specifically, the level of negativity the rater uses in describing the other person and "the simple tendency to see people negatively indicates a greater likelihood of depression and various personality disorders," including narcissism and antisocial behavior.[5] Similarly, how positively we see others correlates with how happy, kindhearted, and emotionally stable we are. Proper (ego-less) perspective gives you the ability to zero in on the good in your world and in others. Our focus becomes our experience, our reality. We decide what is brought into our purview.

Your ego narrates your world, using heuristics to regulate what comes in and what stays out of conscious awareness. The less emotionally healthy someone is, the more they denigrate the world around them to compensate for their own shortcomings and to accommodate their own insecurities. Hence, how someone treats you is a reflection of their own emotional health and says everything about them and nothing about you. We give love. We give respect. If someone doesn't love themselves, what do you expect them to give back? The emotionally healthy person is authentic, true to themselves, and nonjudgmental, accepting of others. The real "I" shines through and their perception of reality is clearer. As a person's self-esteem erodes and their ego engages, their perspective becomes skewed.

Where There's Smoke, There's Fire

Research published in the *Journal of Pediatrics* examined characteristics of various smoke alarms to determine which ones work best to wake children. They found that a sleeping child was about three times more likely to be awakened by an alarm that used their mother's recorded voice than by the typical tone alarm.[6] This response is courtesy of a filtering mechanism located at the base of the brain, the *reticular activating system* (RAS). The RAS keeps us from being overwhelmed by unnecessary stimuli or, in the case of mom's voice in an emergency, ensures that we respond to what's important. Our objectives (and, in some instances, our fears) dictate what we deem important and whether we unconsciously dismiss or consciously accept something.[7]

> ego-based narrative → orients the RAS → filters through heuristics = perspective (what we see and what we think about what we see)

Let's say when conversing at a cocktail party, you become aware of another conversation, and by shifting your attention, you "mute" the person in front of you and pick up what is being said farther away. That's the RAS in action as well. It is powerful, as is what it uncovers. An individual orients their RAS to what is significant—and significance is defined by what they need to see. What they zero in on broadcasts who they are and their perspective on life.

Poker Corner

I said earlier that on the flop (in Texas Hold'em), a player will look briefly at his hole cards and then look away if he's got a strong hand. It's also true that if a player looks

> to his chips after the flop, then he might have a strong hand. The reason is that focus follows interest, and if he wants to bet, then he's going to check to see how much he has and will telegraph his interest by gazing at his chips.

When we take notice of how people see themselves and their world—what attracts their attention and what they avoid; what they mention and what they miss; what they condemn and what they defend; what they accept and what they reject—we know their story of "I." Or put differently, the *what* (they focus on and see) tells you the *why* (they focus on it), and the *why* tells you the *who* (they really are).

As human beings, we seek to make sense of ourselves and our world through stories. And the story that guides our lives is the one that explains "who I am and why I am." This is our *narrative identity,* the "internalized evolving story of the self that we each construct to provide our lives with a sense of purpose and unity."[8] The story of "I" faithfully projects not just who we are, but where we've been and where we're going.

Just like any good story, ours needs a cohesive plot. It needs to make sense. Once we've constructed our narrative, we humans are compelled to maintain it; it's both self-defining and all too self-confining.[9] When a crack appears in our personal narrative, the ego needs to do a quick rewrite to explain *what* is happening and *why.* We create a new story to explain our interpersonal interactions—the behavior of others—as well as explain our own behavior (to ourselves and to others). The ego gives birth to a new narrative. In the next chapter, we will see how we quite literally change our story.

CHAPTER 12

Activating the Defense Grid

When confronted with a discrepancy between our narrative and reality, the ego engages any number of defense mechanisms to distort reality. The integrity of our narrative must be preserved. We lie to ourselves so we can live with ourselves.

None of us wants to admit that we are selfish or lazy, much less a failure or flawed. We need to get our proverbial story straight. The ego is thus equipped with an elaborate array of shields and buffers—*defense mechanisms*—that allow us to reconcile the story of who we are with our behavior. We distort or delete aspects of our world to mitigate their unpleasurable effects from our conscious awareness. The most common of these is avoidance, denial, or justification.

Smoking offers a classic illustration of cognitive dissonance. The smoker may acknowledge that cigarettes cause a wide range of negative health effects, but he probably also desires to be healthy. The tension produced by these inconsistent ideas can be reduced by (a) not thinking about it, (b) disputing or denying the evidence, (c) justifying one's smoking ("A bus could come and hit me tomorrow" or "I need to smoke, or I'd gain too much weight"), or (d) accepting the truth and taking steps to quit (even if repeatedly unsuccessfully). Of course, instead of protecting us (rather than the ego protecting itself), the defense mechanisms displayed in options b and c lead to increased instability and insecurity. As these defenses emerge, the chasm between the truth and our ability to accept it is exposed.

Have you ever wondered why it is so important for someone to believe something despite obvious evidence that it's untrue? He insists that the dictionary is wrong because the word he wants to spell in Scrabble can't be found in it. And playing Trivial Pursuit is a real treat when he has you half-convinced that there is a misprint on every other card. This person "needs" to be right for the same reason someone gets angry. He is unable to feel "less," to be wrong and lose power. A bigger ego means more blame and less personal responsibility and accountability.

This is why it is so hard for someone with low self-esteem to forgive or apologize.[1] Digging in their psychological heels, the ego tricks them into believing that by holding on to their anger, they become powerful and less vulnerable. The opposite is true. If a person is unable to let go, or, even worse, seeks revenge, it is a sign of emotional insolvency. Likewise, how quick are they to apologize when they are wrong or hurt others? Are they able to forgive when they have been hurt? Those who can easily move their ego out of the way—who can forgive and apologize when necessary and appropriate—operate with a higher degree of emotional strength. The eminent psychiatrist Thomas Szasz does not mince words when he writes, "Beware of the person who never says, 'I am sorry.' He is weak and frightened and will, sometimes at the slightest provocation, fight with the desperate ferocity of a cornered animal."[2]

Through the Looking Glass

When it comes to our behavior toward others, the ego is equally equipped to exonerate itself from immoral, selfish, or harmful behavior, which includes: (a) recusal of responsibility ("I was following orders"),

(b) subjective contrast ("Everyone else did X and Y, and I only did X"), or (c) devaluing the victim ("He's not a good person" or "They don't care about people anyway").

We constantly make micro adjustments to our narrative via a *fundamental attribution error*, also known as *correspondence bias* or *attribution effect*. Thus, we are primed to excuse our mistakes or moral lapses by laying blame on the situation or on circumstances beyond our control while ascribing intent or a personality-based explanation for the same behavior in others.[3] A line from the late comedian George Carlin comes to mind: "Have you ever noticed that anybody driving slower than you is an idiot, and anyone going faster than you is a maniac?" True enough, when someone cuts us off in traffic, our first thought is often character-based (e.g., "He's a maniac"; "He's selfish"; "He's unskilled"), instead of attributing his behavior to a situation (e.g., rushing to the hospital or to some other emergency). Conversely, when *we* cut someone off while driving, we assign a noble motive or credit the situation (e.g., "Let's teach this guy a lesson"; "His car came out of nowhere"; "I have an important meeting"; "With the day I had, I deserve to get home quickly to relax"). We believe our actions do not betray anything unseemly about our character.[4]

The greater someone's ego, the more difficult it is for him to see beyond himself and his own wants and needs. Empathy requires a shift in perspective—to put yourself in another person's proverbial shoes. If a person is perpetually self-abosrbed, focused entirely on his own pain, then his ego locks his perspective into place and it is impossible for him to get out of his own way and see through another's lens. When he is in a positive state, he may become inquisitive, seemingly compassionate and interested in the lives of others, but don't be misled. This is only curiosity masquerading as concern.

The Broken Mirror

Most people are not easily offended when faced with a truth that they fully acknowledge, and oftentimes we aren't bothered by a blatant, ridiculous bold-faced lie. It is usually only when presented with a truth that we refuse to accept that we become sensitive or self-conscious. This then leads to fear and the activation of the defense mechanism.

Once we have fully accepted something about ourselves or our lives, we no longer need to hide from it. We don't care who knows about it or who finds out, and we don't allow the reality to hold us back. The truth, once embraced, can never be bruised or injured, yet a delusion can be shattered by a whisper or a glance.

The celebrated psychiatrist Carl Jung writes, "Everything that irritates us about others can lead us to an understanding of ourselves." Many of us are aware that when we are bothered by a fault in others, it is because we share this weakness—at least in some small measure—even if it has never manifested in action. But this does not reveal the entire picture because a person who, for instance, suffers from alcohol addiction may very well be hypersensitive to this trait in others, but whether they become troubled by it is determined by whether they have acted responsibly. In other words, if they see the addiction in themselves, accept it, and have taken responsible action toward recovery, then when they notice the disease in another person, it provokes understanding and empathy, not disdain.[5]

> The greater someone's ego, the more difficult it is for him to see beyond himself and his own wants and needs. Empathy requires a shift in perspective—to put yourself in another person's proverbial shoes.

Hitting a Nerve

Recall that whenever there is a threat to our emotional selves—the lower our self-esteem, in general, and how deeply the truth scores a direct hit on our self-image, in particular—the greater our fear. Our defense grid does not often activate in areas that do not directly attack our self-image. For example, if you are a lousy cook and a person speaks disparagingly about your cooking, the impact is negligible when (a) you accept this fact completely, and (b) you don't see yourself as a cook and, in fact, may even talk with great pride about how you "can't even make toast." However, the closer we get to a person's self-image, the closer we get to the core of their personal narrative: *This is who I am.* This is when the ego will go into overdrive to protect itself.

Take, for example, a professional chef who has low self-esteem. Their entire self-image is on the line with every meal they cook or contest they enter. You can predict the more dominant personality will be loud and controlling, possibly smug and annoying. You know they'll become volatile if things do not go their way. The more passive type will tend to complain, become antagonistic, and appear somewhat dejected. You can also work backward: Seeing a person's response to such a situation will allow you to know more about them.

And what about someone who is hypersensitive to any dissent, much less criticism? A person who is easily and often offended and who becomes vehemently defensive when their opinions, attitudes, and beliefs are questioned is exhibiting that they have exceptionally low self-esteem and an ego that is on constant alert.

The Language of Distance and Detachment

We needn't wait for a person to lash out to know that we have hit a raw nerve. Speech patterns reveal a person's anxiety at the subconscious level and are identified through distancing language. Suppose that a friend of yours is on a diet, and after a holiday break, he states:

STATEMENT A: "The holidays really did me in."
STATEMENT B: "I was not so good over the holidays."

Which statement typefies a person who takes responsibility for his diet, himself, and his life, and which reveals a victim mentality? Note that in the first statement "the holidays" are to blame for his behavior, and in the second he owns his behavior with *I*-language as well as by assuming responsibility for his overeating. The wording may vary, but the pattern of acceptance or deflection remains consistent. Now let's say you probe further as to why he went off his diet:

STATEMENT A: "You just can't eat well with all the food around; diets are impossible on holidays."
STATEMENT B: "I should have brought my own food. I made the mistake of thinking I could have a little bite of everything."

When someone offers a second-person account of one's feelings (as in the first statement) rather than a first-person account of the facts (as in the second statement), this indicates that their ego has clearly activated a distancing mechanism to blunt the emotional pain. Take a look at the following pairs of statements, and note which ones indicate repressed anxiety:

STATEMENT A: "I'm in trouble."
STATEMENT B: "I got myself into trouble."

STATEMENT A: "It's what I think about."
STATEMENT B: "That's where my head goes."

STATEMENT A: "I think these crazy thoughts sometimes."
STATEMENT B: "These crazy thoughts randomly pop into my head."

STATEMENT A: "I'm having difficulty at home."

STATEMENT B: "Things at home are uncomfortable."

The first statements accept responsibility while the second statements recuse the speaker of accountability. Further evidence of detachment (from responsibility) is evident when an individual absorbs himself into a group. A patient, for example, says to the therapist, "You don't care about your patients," rather than, "You don't care about me."[6] The most extreme instance is when the person linguistically deletes both himself and the target of his message. He effectively severs all emotional connection to bring his vulnerability to zero, stating, "Analysts don't care about their patients."[7]

> Detachment is the nuclear option of defense mechanisms for dealing with either suppressed or repressed anxiety.

Other detachment mechanisms employ intellectualizing and conceptualizing one's feelings. For example, a psychiatrist asks a patient to describe how she felt when her mother abandoned her at a young age. The patient responds, "I was really hurt when my mother left." This appears to be an honest and healthy expression of her feelings. If she were unable to acknowledge the pain, her response would sound more like:

- "That would be tough for any child."
- "You know, life isn't easy for too many people."
- "You learn to grow up quick."

Detachment is the nuclear option of defense mechanisms for dealing with either suppressed or repressed anxiety. When the pain is too intense, the "I" leaves to cope with overwhelming emotions. For this reason, people in extreme grief don't use the typical pronouns of self-absorption (*I, me,* and *my*). Sadness, even clinical depression, shifts our awareness toward ourselves. Intense grief, on the other hand, is channeled away from the self. Requiring an emotional shock absorber, we don't take in the raw emotion. This is akin to the experience of extreme anger, where we avoid personal pronouns, opting instead for seemingly impersonal, distant, or matter-of-fact language.

Taking note when we are digging near a raw nerve can help assess another person's fear and insecurities, but knowing in advance which areas are the most sensitive can be invaluable. Although the values that we hold announce to the world what matters to us, we are about to see how the qualitative nature of our values unveils a self-portrait of our deepest selves.

CHAPTER 13

The Meaning of Values

When people talk or write about themselves, they generally emphasize one of five domains. They speak in terms of their character traits (e.g., "I'm honest"; "I'm friendly"; "I'm hardworking"), their relationships (e.g., "I'm the father of three amazing girls"; "I enjoy good friends"), their possessions (e.g., "I own a home by the lake"; "I love to tool around in my refurbished '67 Mustang"), their physical attributes (e.g., "I have an athletic build"; "I have light blue eyes and blond hair"), or their profession or skill set (e.g., "I'm an architect"; "I'm good with my hands"). In this respect, you can effectively detect themes that reveal a person's self-image—how they see themselves, what they value in themselves, and also what they believe makes them valuable to others.

Logic informs us that the same traits we value in ourselves are the ones we value in others. The individual who prides himself on his physical fitness is inclined to admire those same qualities in others. To him, this is meaningful and makes someone worthy of esteem and connection. Plug in any trait. A person who is punctual, even to a fault, holds punctuality to be virtuous.[1] It's essential to qualify that only those traits and characteristics that we value in ourselves are the ones we admire and are similarly attracted to in others. A morbidly obese hoarder does not likely admire those traits if he himself is unhappy with his lot.

Likewise, the always-late, egocentric executive will not think kindly of being kept waiting himself.

The dual takeaway here is that whatever quality someone is preoccupied with or focused on in their own life, they are likely paying disproportionate attention to it in you. Likewise, when you know what someone is particularly alert to in others, you gain an insight into what they themselves value. As C. W. Lewis observes, "Just as men spontaneously praise whatever they value, so they spontaneously urge us to join them in praising it: 'Isn't she lovely? Wasn't it glorious? Don't you think that magnificent?'"[2]

Take note of how people steer the conversation or perhaps switch the topic completely. Back in the day, when Cadillac was, well, the Cadillac of cars, a business acquaintance of mine found it necessary to insert into every conversation the fact that he owned such a car. I recall him shaking hands with a new colleague and wasting no time. "Nice handshake, kid. My car dealer has a handshake like that." Pause. Then we were treated to the make and model of said car.

A person who lacks what they feel is valuable is going to be hypersensitive in this area. In the case of my business acquaintance, his constant need to mention an expensive possession—his Cadillac—spoke to his insecurity about having enough money. Whatever the value, the ego will seek to portray and project this image, and his degree of self-esteem becomes illuminated when the said value is called into question. Recall from the last chapter that when there is a threat to a person's emotional self, the lower their self-esteem and the closer the threat is to their self-image, the more the underbelly of their personal narrative is exposed—and the further their ego moves into overdrive to shield itself.

The Value of Meaning

Authentic, sustainable happiness—let alone mental health—is found in our connection to reality, not in our escape from it. The more meaning something has, the greater the inherent pleasure it brings. Lying on the couch and watching TV is undoubtedly comfortable but hardly meaningful. The pursuit of comfort is basically the avoidance of life and not only denies us genuine pleasure but also short-circuits the entirety of our well-being.

Make no mistake, the pursuit of ego-oriented objectives takes us out of reality as completely and as quickly as the pursuit of amusement and recreation. Eminent psychologist and Holocaust survivor Viktor Frankl describes this as "an unheard cry for meaning," and Sigmund Freud writes, "It is impossible to escape the impression that people commonly use false standards of measurement—that they seek power, success, and wealth for themselves and admire them in others, and that they underestimate what is of true value in life."[3]

Studies confirm that those who place a high priority on money and fame are significantly less happy and emotionally solvent than those who strive to bring meaning into their lives by pursuing healthy relationships, developing their potential, and becoming involved in social causes.[4] It's not that having money or fame *make you unhappy*. Not at all. You *can* have these things and also be happy, but happiness is not contingent on these things. Indeed, being comfortable and having fun are not enough. Our deepest self gnaws at us—not just to do more but to become something more as well. In the words of Abraham Maslow, "If you plan on being anything less than you are capable of being, you will probably be unhappy and angry all of the days of your life."[5]

The axis of psychology has long consisted of the following theories regarding our motivation: Sigmund Freud (we are motivated by pleasure), Alfred Adler (we are motivated by power), and

> Whatever quality someone is preoccupied with or focused on in their own life, they are likely paying disproportionate attention to it in you. Likewise, when you know what someone is particularly alert to in others, you gain an insight into what they themselves value.

meaning theory (we strive primarily to find meaning). We can see how these three models synthesize into a single construct. The pursuit of meaning gives us maximum pleasure, the prerequisite of which is self-regulation, or the ability to maintain control over oneself. This is the highest form of power.

Self-Esteem, Impulse Control, and Emotional Health

We now come full circle. The fuel required to live one's life with meaning—consistent with one's true values—requires impulse control: the ability to say no to one's self. If you don't like yourself, however, you are not going to invest in yourself. Period. Self-esteem—which is self-love—stimulates the desire and energy for self-discipline. When self-esteem is low, our interest and attention shift from long term to immediate gratification—if it feels good, do it and damn the consequences. Our short-term focus is shallow and narrow. Countless studies show the link between low self-esteem and a range of self-destructive behaviors and habits, from compulsive gambling, gaming, and shopping, to impulsive and risky activities, to outright self-harm.

When we love ourselves, we can invest in our long-term satisfaction and well-being with maximum effort and minimal pain. Similarly, when we love someone, we want to give to that person, and when we love ourselves, we want to give to ourselves. We can do so easily because we're not focused on the effort (aka pain) but on the reward (aka pleasure). How we feel about ourselves defines the entirety of the experience. The pain or effort involved in any task is felt only in contrast to the level of self-esteem.

When someone does not feel good about himself, he will often seek the temporary, hollow refuge of immediate gratification and give in to impulses instead of rising above them. The vapor-like pleasure masking his contempt for himself quickly dissipates because the comfort sought is replaced by greater pain. He only cycles lower and lower. As we seek to avoid the pain of legitimate challenges, we are in essence avoiding a meaningful and, thus, pleasurable life.

Who Pays the Price

Personality disorders and affective disorders are by no means mutually exclusive. But someone suffering from a personality disorder is going to reduce their personal pain by inflicting it on others. A lack of impulse control that leads to a gambling debt, for example, may result in an attempt to manipulate others to come to his rescue. Some may resort to crime or violence to ease their burden.

With or without a personality disorder, those suffering from an affective disorder are more prone to openly self-destruct via any number of vices. To gain a reprieve from their pain, they will turn to whatever means of distraction and diversion are available. They punish themselves in ways disguised as pleasure—excessive eating, binge drinking, drug abuse, and endless other distractions—to keep from examining their lives. They want to love themselves, but they lose themselves instead. They are unable to invest in their well-being, so they substitute illusions for love. Over time—and to varying degrees of self-awareness—as the guilt and shame compounds, self-sabotage turns into self-harm. They no longer seek to escape pain but to inflict it on themselves.

Why do some people cope with stress and trauma better than others? The answer is resilience. In the next chapter, we will dive more deeply into the intricacies of self-esteem, impulse control, and anxiety. When we understand how different people respond to life's stressors, we will be able to predict who will bend and who will break.

CHAPTER 14

The Resilience Factor

While circumstances affect our mental health, the ability to rise above challenges and bounce back is the factor that dictates how much impact external events have on us. Emotional resilience means the capacity to adapt to and cope with stress and to overcome adversity without becoming psychologically dysfunctional (such as slipping into a persistent negative mood or true, clinical depression). You can think of resilience as emotional Teflon coating, a kind of hardiness that not only helps us cope with the stresses of everyday life but also protects us when we're confronted by significant stressors or traumas.

Less Ego = Less Need to Control

Emotional resilience is born out of a belief in ourselves and a belief in something beyond ourselves. There is not always a *why* that we (the ego part) can understand from our limited perspective. Once we are willing to accept this, we no longer need to make sense of the unknowable. Of course, the ego cannot allow this. It needs to forge the unknowns—of every size and impact—into knowns. It is forever grasping at illogical straws in a futile attempt to explain the unexplainable. Our resilience is keyed to the acknowledgment that some of life's most painful ordeals are beyond our comprehension. If we accept or, better still, embrace, the unknown—and that although we cannot fathom the why, we know it is geared toward our ultimate good—then we move toward emotional resiliency. If we allow our ego to get the better of us, then every bump and bruise is met with angry defiance, reinforcing the ego's message that we are bad and deserving of pain and punishment.

The more egocentric a person is, the more the world revolves around him and, due to low self-esteem, the more he believes himself deserving of pain and hardship. Thus, he concludes that everything is done *to* him—not *for* him, for some greater good—because, from his perspective, the universe (and everyone in it) hates him. The egocentric individual personalizes everything. It rains on his camping trip because he's not allowed to have a good time. The eight-car pileup that made him late for his meeting is similarly orchestrated to get back at him. It's all about him. As egocentricity expands, the person may become paranoid and believe himself to be the epicenter of causation for all that happens.

We All Flee to Some Degree

Everywhere you turn, there are convenient vehicles for mindless distraction. Instant entertainment offers escape into other worlds, a never-ending labyrinth of video games, movies, TV shows, blogs, and forums where we can dissociate from life's stressors. Each and every time we tune out rather than face the proverbial music, our resiliency gets dinged.

When the constant chatter of the mind—the worries, fears, and anxieties—cannot be turned off, we tune out. We mute the uncomfortable noise of self-reflection and raise the volume of illusion. Scrolling through millions of Twitter feeds, researchers have found that users who suffer from depression frequently write about modes of distraction and escapism. Among the most recurring words are: *watch, movie time, episode, read, season, totally, book, favorite play, character, awesome, scene, star, stuff, cool, horror,* and *start.*[1]

Psychologist and marketing guru Ernest Dichter, known as the "father of motivational research," explains that when human beings become fearful, most will regress to soothing, even infantile, behaviors and animalistic drives to distract themselves from, and channel, their anxiety.[2] This is the psychology behind the typically high-sugar, fat-saturated, or salt-laden go-to "comfort foods." They provide a feeling of fullness instead of emptiness and tend to elevate our mood (albeit briefly). They create a short-lived feeling of well-being by stimulating the brain's reward system, which temporarily dampens emotional distress.

This observation is particularly useful because it reveals how people manage stress in their lives in general. *Terror management theory* explains that we deal with anxiety in one of two ways. When we are living full and robust lives, we tend to embrace our values and beliefs—that which brings meaning into our lives. This is known as the *mortality salience hypothesis* and promotes self-regulation. But if we are living less-than-meaningful lives, we pacify our fears with self-indulgence—from chocolate to vacations. This is known as the *anxiety-buffer hypothesis.*[3] Ever wonder why the ads during the evening news are often for products that enable escapism? Studies have found that news of disaster and death makes viewers shift to a mentality of "Let us eat and drink; for tomorrow we shall die."[4] In other words, sad news makes you want to indulge—and to seek immediate gratification. The Achilles' heel of impulse control lies in how we manage our fears. This is valuable to understand because in any number of scenarios—such as a date, negotiation, or interview—how people typically respond to anxiety-provoking situations echoes their mental health.[5] Do they see, accept, and respond;

> In any number of scenarios—such as a date, negotiation, or interview—how people typically respond to anxiety-provoking situations echoes their mental health.

react and then regret; or just plain duck and hide? When we're confronted with a stressor, we appraise the situation, then decide how to respond. Taking breaks from your work, for example, is a good thing. However, if you have anxiety about the work, those breaks should prompt you to work through anxiety, not avoid it. If you close the laptop and walk away during a wave of anxiety, you reinforce a pattern of escapism. Flee, and you temporarily lessen the anxiety but reinforce the neural pattern that avoidance brings calm and comfort. That calm is short-lived because it is soon replaced with guilt, which is anger turned inward.

The anger and anxiety loop continues to reinforce itself. Among the most important triggers of self-regulation failure—what makes us lose self-control and give in to our impulses—is anger.[6] Predictably, anger gives way to a range of self-destructive behavior and habits, such as alcoholism, gambling, and drug addiction.[7]

Have you ever noticed that when you are angry with yourself, you are more prone to bang into things or knock them over? That's emotional discombobulation—being angry with yourself—manifesting physically. Maybe you're flushed and distracted and so you literally didn't see that table. But it's also psychologically probable that you're experiencing an unconscious attempt to punish yourself because you made a decision that you knew was not right, even though you could not help yourself at the time. More simply put: Guilt is a negative force that weighs us down, causing us to engage in unconsciously motivated self-destructive behavior. According to a study of more than 2,500 patients who had been seriously injured and sought care in the emergency room, researchers found that 31.7 percent reported some degree of irritability just before the injury, 18.1 percent reported feeling angry, and 13.2 percent reported feeling hostile.[8]

The Over-/Under-

The quality of our emotional lives is directly proportional to the amount of responsibility we are willing to accept. In *Reality Therapy*, renowned psychiatrist Dr. William Glasser writes: "People do not act irresponsibly because they are ill; they are ill because they act irresponsibly."[9] But how do we measure authentic responsibility? The question is not as simple as you might assume—because people who suffer from a personality disorder will either undercontrol or overcontrol their impulses. What looks like robust emotional health and strong conviction to moral values and ideals may be something else entirely.

There's an age-old riddle that asks, "How far can you go into a forest?" The answer is *halfway* because after you reach the middle, you're beginning to come out. In gauging emotional well-being, we're often looking for the middle of the forest—balance and moderation. When exhibited in the extreme, practically any attitude or behavior, no matter how admirable or reasonable, begins to drift into that gnarly thicket of being unhealthy.

For example, cleanliness is a virtue, unless someone becomes so obsessed with being clean that they clean constantly, frantically, and compulsively, to the point that they are cleaning things that were already clean. Having a degree of openness and receptiveness is a positive and healthy trait, of course; so is being appropriately cautious and reserved. But when we move into either extreme, we're drifting into unhealthy territory. Likewise, dedication to exercise is a positive, healthy attribute; however, running with a broken foot because you feel you must "get your exercise in" is clearly not a good sign. The behavior is dangerous and represents neither discipline nor wisdom but its opposite—foolishness and a lack of self-restraint. Almost any admirable trait has an unhealthy counterpart:

- Being affectionate is positive, while being distant or indifferent is not—yet being too clingy is unhealthy.

- Showing courage is positive, while cowering is not—yet being brazen is unhealthy.
- · Having determination is positive, while being indecisive and unsure is not—yet close-mindedness is unhealthy.
- Being flexible is positive, while being rigid and stubborn is not—yet not having a backbone is unhealthy.
- Trusting others is positive, while being paranoid is not—yet being too naive is unhealthy.

A lack of impulse control can manifest as frequent disregard for both oneself and others. Does someone pay their credit card bills on time and live within their means? Or are they careless or irresponsible with their money? Are they thoughtful and calculating in their decisions? Or do they engage in high-risk behavior, demonstrate poor judgment, and exhibit recklessness with their own safety and that of others? Do they think things through and consider the consequences? Or would they be described as someone who makes rash and brash decisions?

At the same time, we want to pay attention to extremes, such as a person who is incapable of taking responsible risks and investing in themselves. A rigid and persistent overcontrol of oneself may signal a hidden personality disorder. Those with avoidant personality disorder, for example, are afraid of venturing into social settings for fear of ridicule or scorn. Similarly, people suffering from an obsessive-compulsive personality disorder operate with an intense fear of being bad or wrong. As such, their overactive conscience drives them to be overly scrupulous and hyperfocused on rules and regulations. This is true in every domain. There are those who challenge authority at every turn because they have no respect for it, let alone social norms. At the same time, there are those who are afraid to bend or break even the most minor rule because they fear the consequences and have a disproportionate fear of authority.

Much more goes into the psychological mix, because not only are there many classifications of mental illness but also a mind-numbing number of gradations. The challenge of identifying the problem is further compounded because they often intertwine or overlap, with a comorbidity rate of 90 percent.[10] When a person has one personality disorder, they are likely to have at least one additional personality disorder as well as an increased likelihood of anxiety and depression.

In part IV, my profiling system allows you to tell whether someone is emotionally unwell without you having to assume a formal diagnosis. It is designed to offer insight into a person's mental framework, not label them with a specific illness or disorder (although we will zero in on certain conditions). This gives you the ability to know how far an individual deviates from being emotionally healthy rather than pathologizing their symptoms into one immutable diagnosis.

PART IV

BUILDING A PSYCHOLOGICAL PROFILE

If you're concerned about a new relationship or even an old one, you will no longer need to guess what's going on and what may go very wrong. Even when your interaction with someone is limited to mere observation or a brief exchange—whether you're on a Zoom call, at the park, or even in an elevator—this section will help you crack open the window into a person's psyche and view anyone's emotional stability. You'll learn how to tell if a person is normal, neurotic, or far more dangerous—in person, online, or even over the phone.

CHAPTER 15

In Search of Sanity

Perspective determines how we see and respond to any situation and guides us (or deceives us) to place it in one of two categories—"it matters" or "it doesn't matter." Picking the low-hanging fruit of a psychological assessment requires us to answer the following questions: Does this person have a balanced outlook on life's priorities? Or does he blow little things out of proportion, while perhaps ignoring the main things? Does he seem to know what is important and what is not? Or does he live in a perpetual state of chaos and crisis, where there is always something going on? Does she have an attitude of gratitude or expectation? Or is she a constant blamer and complainer? Does he enjoy life despite the occasional setback? Or is he just waiting for the next disaster to happen?

If you notice that someone is constantly agitated over little things (and excited over the trivial), pay attention. To the emotionally unwell person, every little thing is a big thing. Think about it. In any situation where you lack perspective, you have no way to tell whether or not something matters. Perspective provides context, and context allows for meaning. Without context there is no recognition of, much less appreciation for, our challenges.

A great deal is revealed by how someone responds to life's little losses and wins. But we do not need to wait and watch. Everyday conversation also provides a magnifying glass into a person's inner world.

The Lens of Reality

An identifiable marker for perspective is revealed by how someone responds to, and reflects on, life's challenging experiences and even routine circumstances. Our perspective is typified by whether we organize our experiences through themes of *contamination* or *redemption*. The latter correlates with greater emotional well-being, and the former with poorer mental health.[1]

> If you notice that someone is constantly agitated over little things (and excited over the trivial), pay attention. To the emotionally unwell person, every little thing is a big thing.

A contamination narrative is one where "everything is ruined" because of X and the positive inevitably gives way to the negative and becomes irrevocably spoiled or ruined.[2] Unable to extract any good—let alone view the event as "positive" on balance— this person paints the entire experience with a stained brush (e.g., "It rained halfway through the picnic, and everything got ruined").[3] No thought or mention of any laughter, joy, and conversation up until that point; no talk of reconnecting with an old friend. Any good might be briefly acknowledged and then quickly minimized or mitigated. All sweetness is soured. The totality of the event is recast into a negative experience and recollected as such.

In contrast, a redemptive narrative is when we dig deeply to mine the silver lining, even when the situation has an objectively difficult or sad ending. This is not, of course, to say that we look back fondly on every difficulty or feel that, on balance, the good outweighed the bad. Rather, we are able to frame a significant hardship (e.g., a personal trauma or illness of a loved one) as the catalyst that ultimately delivers redemption or sweetness (e.g., bringing together family; shifting one's perspective to reprioritize one's values).[4] We can also recognize pockets of positivity that foster gratitude (e.g., there was no pain; the staff was caring; we were surrounded by family).

When a person speaks about his life, the mere ratio and density of positive to negative details and events further unearth his perspective.[5] Intuitively, we recognize that someone's emphasis on the negative speaks to contamination themes, while his emphasis on the positive speaks to redemptive themes. We all know someone who can walk into a room and find the one thing that isn't perfect. He zeros in on it like a moth to the flame. This is his reality. Negative. By extension, we know that he is generally ungrateful, joyless, and in his interpersonal relationships has a "What have you done for me lately?" attitude.

People who share a common worldview have similar language patterns. We are about to see that those who lack perspective speak a language all their own.

Absolutely, Positively, 100 Percent

In chapter 11, we learned that to feed the illusion of security, the ego is quick to orient our worldview with foregone conclusions and categories. Individuals with a high level of repressed anxiety have a high frequency of dogmatic expressions that feature words such as *always, everybody, nobody, totally, necessary,* and *surely.* In contrast, individuals with a low level of anxiety are able to express a more nuanced position by using words such as *sometimes, rarely, perhaps, almost,* and *maybe.*[6]

In specific instances, the more anxious we are, the more we seek to paper over our insecurities with childlike optimism and certitude. A surgeon is asked, "He's going to be okay, right?" versus "What's the prognosis?" Intuitively, we know that the first question comes from a scared and concerned party, while the other is from one who is less so. Likewise, which of the following Google searches would be conducted by someone who has already invested in Bitcoin or who very much wants to?

(a) Will Bitcoin go to $100,000?
(b) Will Bitcoin go up this year?
(c) Is Bitcoin a good investment?
(d) Which cryptocurrency will do best over the next year?
(e) Which is the safest investment: cryptocurrency, stocks, or real estate?

The language of each search tells us who is open to different investment options, who is leaning in one direction, and who has made up her mind and is looking for confirmation that she is correct. In general, the less grounded a person feels, the more she needs to paint her world in black and white.[7] The shape of her own identity becomes fortified by hardening the lines of the world around her.

A lack of perspective is typified by absolutist thinking, which is mirrored in someone's speech.[8] Words, expressions, or ideas that denote or symbolize totality (in magnitude or probability) or extremism in behavior or beliefs are considered "absolute."[9]

Absolutes (e.g., *all, everything, complete*)

Absolute negatives (e.g., *never, nothing, nobody*)

Absolutists typically extrapolate from a single incidence to *always* because they lack perspective and subsequent context to see the full picture. They also need to be right, which means that coherence trumps truth.

> In general, the less grounded a person feels, the more she needs to paint her world in black and white. The shape of her own identity becomes fortified by hardening the lines of the world around her.

Their ability to make associations fit their narratives is nothing short of staggering. Observe how often the person engages in selective memory, like a child who says, "You never let me . . . ," as opposed to the healthier and more balanced variation: "Sometimes you don't let me . . ." Another common example might include: "If I don't get this, I'll never be happy . . ."

Intensifiers: Turning Up the Heat

The use of abrasive language is characteristic of absolutism. Rather than making a simple, accurate claim, such as "This clock isn't working anymore," someone says, "The clock is busted to pieces!" It's an almost childlike perspective that evokes the image of a tantrum, during which the clock has been thrown around the room and destroyed. Consider the statements "I really blistered my knee to ribbons" and "My performance has completely devastated the team." They exhibit both absolute (black-or-white) tendencies and violent, harsh, or overstated language. "We got into a little tiff" or "We see things differently" is quite different from "We had a huge blowout" or "We went to war over the schedule." Gradations abound:

> You broke the thing.
> You busted the thing.
> You busted the whole thing.
> You completely busted the whole thing.
> You completely busted the whole entire damn thing.

A person's language pattern is revealing of their personality, and should mental illness emerge, the inevitable trajectory to either *ego-dystonic* or *ego-syntonic* disorders (see chapter 10 for a refresher on these terms). The emotionally unwell submissive type is equally disposed to using intensifiers but with language that is more in line with a docile, even refined, nature. This produces a language pattern whereby "I ripped him to pieces in the interview" may sound more like "I was at my most wonderful best." Sampling a nice ripe apple, the dominant type may declare, "This is the best f—king apple," and the submissive type will voice something more akin to "This is the most glorious apple I ever ate in my entire life" or "I could go mad from eating these apples."

The use of expletives is similar to that of absolutist words because they commonly work as adverbial intensifiers.[10] Instead of saying or writing, "I'm completely sick of this," a person may instead replace the absolutist word *completely* with a more forceful adverbial intensifier akin to "I'm f—king sick of this."[11]

Certainly, a person is, at times, entitled to speak emphatically and use sweeping terms and generalities in anger or excitement. By definition, such instances are indicative of a narrowed perspective, and the language accurately signals an individual's state. This is normal and understandable. The use of absolute language, like all grammatical indicators, is best observed by noting *frequency, duration, intensity,* and *context* to determine if such behavior points to a trait and is declarative of someone's overall perspective and thus mental health.

To note that something takes place every day, for example, is not considered absolutist if it does indeed occur every day. For instance, "Every day, I do the best I can" is a world away from "Every single damn day, I do every possible thing I f—king can."

Context is important, too. The language that one uses to claim victory in a professional sports match, an intraoffice Ping-Pong game, or a local Bake-Off will understandably vary, and touting "complete and total annihilation over those losers" with utter seriousness is less troubling in the context of the WWF than the other two. Similarly, a person in authority or perhaps one under a time constraint is under no obligation to sugarcoat an opinion or response, and in such instances, there may be good reason for her to speak in sweeping terms or be excessively blunt. Yet outside of these dynamics, the escalating pattern of judge, jury, and executioner is revealing. When "I don't like cold weather" becomes "No one likes cold weather" or "Only idiots like cold weather," we learn a lot more about this person than his dislike for the cold.

The Judge, Jury, and Executioner

Someone may very well have busted the entire clock. This statement may or may not be true, as many other expressions of facts and feelings (e.g., "I never drive in rushhour traffic"; "Mondays are always my worst day"). But absolute language morphs into more pronounced signals of emotional disturbance when our personal assessment, opinion, or judgment becomes not only absolute but also universal. It should come as no surprise that these language patterns are built on the chassis of egocentricity and the accompanying narrow perspective and low self-esteem.

Level 1: Judge

When someone is speaking from a "judge" perspective, they are essentially projecting their own perspective as objective reality (e.g., "This is the best place to vacation"; "Everyone likes warm weather"; "One cannot manage one's day without a calendar"; "No one likes super-sweet desserts"). The "judge" excludes statements that reflect generally accepted and universal likes and dislikes (e.g., "No one likes to be taken advantage of").

Level 2: Judge and Jury

A more troubling perspective distortion is when one becomes judge and jury, both passing judgment and imprinting a moral stamp that labels the *goodness* or the *badness* of a person, place, or idea (e.g., "Anyone who likes hot weather is crazy"; "You're a fool if you don't use an organizer"). Recall that the ego secures its footing through the use of definitive conclusions and wide-sweeping categories. Judgmental adjectives (e.g., *good, dumb, obvious, maddening*) serve both to ground the ego and offer either moral superiority or justification for one's actions.

Level 3: Judge, Jury, and Executioner

Here a person advocates for retribution or justice against those who do not see the world through his lens or who contrary to his desires and expectations (e.g., "Anyone who doesn't like 'X' is an idiot and should be locked away").

Within each level, a verbal intensifier will magnify the distortion. In level 3, for instance, there is a striking distinction between "Anyone who doesn't like sports is an idiot and should be locked away," and "Anyone who doesn't like sports is a raging idiot and should be shot in his damn stupid head." Both of these statements indicate a more dominant personality. A persistent pattern of this language personifies an *ego-syntonic* disorder. The submissive counterpart would sound more like, "I want zero to do with people who aren't art lovers and they should all live far away from humanity." The sentiment remains, but the aggression is muted. We already know that we can't make a snap judgment based on one sentence, but sometimes a small grammatical detail bares rich insight, and we may want to probe further when necessary. Once again, *factoring frequency, duration, intensity,* and *context* will differentiate state from trait.[12]

I'll illustrate with an unfolding dialogue. After taking a bite of dessert, Jane declares aloud, "This is the best cake I've ever tasted." Such a statement is dramatic, but we will allow for the possibility that it may be factual. However, stating "This will be the best cake you've ever tasted" morphs an opinion—which is, by definition, subjective—into a fact and moves Jane into the sphere of judgment. After sampling the dessert, Hana replies, "It's not bad." As Hana's response lacks both proper enthusiasm and confirmation of her "fact," Jane becomes annoyed: "You don't know what you're talking about!" Jane's inability to recognize that her taste buds might not represent all of humanity's is telling—and more so should she designate Hana to be not just wrong but also a bad person because she holds a different opinion.

We are all entitled to our likes and dislikes, and may believe that others should see things the way that we do. The less healthy a person is, however, the more they *need* for others to adopt their worldview as their own.[13] In Jane's case, there is little gray area where opposing ideas and beliefs can coexist, because they represent existential threats to her values and belief system—the DNA of her narrative identity. Whatever she holds to be true *is* who she is and must be protected at all costs.[14] This is who she is, and if you don't like what she likes, then you don't like her. If you don't believe as she does, then, in her egocentricity, whoever is wrong will cease to exist—and it's not going to be her.

Let's look more deeply into her psyche.

Every Picture Paints a Story

Dining in a restaurant, a person finds their server to be less than friendly. The healthiest perspective is to not take it personally and presume that perhaps she is having a hard day or has a hard life. Either way, the diner is focused on the server's pain and not his own. Remember, however, that a person in emotional pain becomes perpetually self-absorbed. His ego locks his perspective into place, and he cannot get out of his own way and see through another's lens. The following sentiments appear in descending order of gradations of the diner's emotional state and, if the sentiment is part of a pattern, speaks to his overall emotional health:

- The waitress is rude.
- All the waitresses in this place are rude.
- No one in the service industry has any manners.
- Rude people are what's wrong with this country.
- Rude people should be shot.

The pain is intolerable for the person who consistently voices sentiments echoing the fifth response. Outright disrespect or invalidation cuts straight to their core because it is internalized as disconnection, "reminding them" of their utter unworthiness.

Each circumstance we encounter is like a blank book until we write the script with our thoughts. For instance, when someone acts rudely toward us, it doesn't mean anything. This person's words or deeds cause us to feel bad about ourselves (or not) because of our self-image. What does their opinion really have to do with our self-worth? Nothing. But that's just what the ego does—it makes everything about us.

The greater our self-esteem, the slower we are to take offense. When we love ourselves, (a) we don't assume that someone's actions mean they don't respect us, and (b) even if we do come to that conclusion, we aren't emotionally unsettled because we don't need their love or respect in order to feel worthy. We are not in pain, because we do not fear disconnection. We are unharmed and then free to recognize the basis for the other person's behavior—that is, their own feelings of inadequacy and insecurity.

As self-esteem erodes and the ego engages, we become hyperalert for anything and anyone who may injure us. We remain on the lookout for any situation that calls into question our worth, fearful that we are not loved and lovable. But this is not simply about vigilance. When the ego is engaged, it means that we are actively focused on the negative. Inevitably, we conclude that all negative experiences are due to a deficiency within ourselves. We draw conclusions that do not mitigate our insecurities and vulnerabilities but instead feed them. We are looking for signs that we are not worthy of love and respect. If we don't find these signs, we may convince ourselves that we *have* found them, even in benign comments and happenstance, so that this interpretation fits our narrative.

We connect the dots of someone else's behavior to affirm our deepest fear: *I am unworthy*. Cue anger. Lack of self-worth causes an out-of-proportion response or situation in which we feel disrespected or unloved. The world, funneled through the ego, is our only source of psychological nourishment. When we feel we're not getting the respect we crave, anger and cognitive distortions engage to defend against our feelings of vulnerability.

Self-esteem and the ego are inversely related. To the degree that we suffer from low self-esteem, the ego swells and our perspective narrows; like a seesaw, when one goes up, the other goes down. A person's emotional health is sensibly assessed by observing their perspective and self-esteem. In the next chapter, we will see what real self-esteem looks like and why it is so easily confused with confidence and bravado.

CHAPTER 16

The Psychology of Self-Esteem

Self-esteem is often confused with confidence, but the two are quite different, and making the distinction is important. Confidence is how effective we feel within a specific area or situation, while self-esteem is the recognition that we are loved and lovable and feel worthy of receiving good in our lives. An emotionally healthy person may feel good about herself (have self-esteem) yet not feel certain that she will succeed in certain situations (be unconfident about her skill set). For instance, someone who has high self-esteem may be a poor chess player, but she still likes herself. She will exhibit signs of decreased confidence when playing chess with a superior player, yet her overall sense of self-worth remains unaffected.

Certainly, someone who attempts to fortify his self-image by placing great emphasis on a specific trait may exhibit signs of higher self-esteem to the untrained eye, but he in effect suffers from very low self-esteem because he has built an entire identity around an inborn talent or nurtured skill. *I am significant because I am pretty; I am valuable because I am smart.* This view of worthiness is defined by an egocentric mindset that forces him to pit himself against others—constantly comparing, judging, and inevitably condemning—in order to feel worthy of love and connection.

A person's inflated ego does not derive from extremely high levels of self-esteem but rather from self-loathing.[1] Don't fall into the trap of believing that a person with an inflated ego likes himself; ego and self-esteem are inversely related. No matter how much a person appears to be happy with himself, if he is egocentric, that person suffers from feelings of inferiority.

Running like the Devil

The ego is the false self and exists only to compensate for feelings of guilt or inferiority—aspects of the self that we are unable to love, to accept. Arrogance is a manifestation of the ego that fosters attitudes, beliefs, and values to bolster a faltering self-image. It is confirmation of low self-esteem.

An arrogant person never feels whole, complete. He is an emotional junkie, depending on others to feed his fragile ego—he's a slave to his own impulses, which he cannot rise above. It's too easy to mistake humility for weakness, but humility, in fact, signifies strength and a high level of self-esteem.[2] When a person has humility, he is fulfilled.[3] Humility allows us to exercise self-control, and we only gain self-esteem—the central key to psychological health—when we are able to make responsible choices, regardless of what we feel like doing or how it appears to others.

On the surface, it may appear that an arrogant person is fueled by so much self-esteem that he is fearless when, in fact, he is

> Don't fall into the trap of believing that a person with an inflated ego likes himself; ego and self-esteem are inversely related. No matter how much a person appears to be happy with himself, if he is egocentric, that person suffers from feelings of inferiority.

driven by a larger fear that simply eclipses the more immediate fear. The person is still scared of X (i.e., looking foolish, being rejected, failing), but the deeper fear of Y (i.e., poverty, not being famous, or whatever makes him feel like a greater failure) forces him to act in spite of his momentary fear.[4]

This personality type presents an attitude of confidence, defiance, and self-righteousness, but his surface behavior doesn't reveal the ego's true fragility—namely, the need for recognition and respect. If this person wishes to amass a great fortune, for example, he may certainly run roughshod over others, with obvious disregard of making a favorable impression. Nonetheless, his ego-based drive is ultimately a societal-based pursuit—one that will leave him perpetually lacking—because he depends on others to tell him when he has achieved success. So brazen on the outside yet so brittle on the inside. No matter how successful he becomes, he will never feel accomplished.

The Myth of the Self-Loving Narcissist

It is a pervasive myth that narcissism is the result of having too much self-esteem. Although narcissism is often defined as extreme self-love, it is, in fact, born out of extreme self-hatred. Narcissus is the origin of the term *narcissism*, defined as a fixation with oneself and one's physical appearance or one's public perception. In Greek mythology, Narcissus was a hunter known for his beauty. His modern relatives, the narcissists, focus on externalities and the false "I," which as we know, speaks not just to their mindsets but to their mental health.

An analysis of linguistic markers of narcissism underscores the origin of this pathology and illustrates this trait. One of the strongest correlations with narcissism is a propensity for using profanity.[5] This is due to a hyperfocus on physicality and sexuality—swear words invariably involve a body part, bodily function, or physical act. Once again, frequency, duration, intensity, and context must be considered. Infrequent, context-relevant vulgarity is hardly suggestive of anything more than uncouth frustration expressing itself. Immature? Yes. Pathological? No.

The widespread belief that narcissism provides a reservoir of emotional resiliency in the face of adversity is plainly incorrect. Research finds the opposite: Narcissists have increased physiological reactivity to emotional distress (activation of the fight-flight-freeze response) and stress-response systems that are particularly susceptible to everyday frustrations.[6] Narcissists have an elevated output of two biomarkers of stress—cortisol and alpha-amylase—in response to the experience of negative emotions.[7] In plain English: They have a lower boiling point. Although they are more easily ruffled, they may do a superior job of masking—and, to varying degrees, repressing—their fears and insecurities.

Narcissists don't often use language that is related to anxiety and fear (e.g., *afraid, distraught, horror*).[8] They are also less tentative in their language (and, therefore, less likely to use words such as *maybe, probably, hopefully, perhaps,* and *guess*).[9] Again, when we understand the psychology, the reasoning emerges. Their language projects strength to compensate for weakness.[10] A person with a faltering self-image has a linguistic profile that projects confidence with definitive language to conceal intolerable vulnerabilities and insecurities.[11] Predictably, the belief systems of highly anxious people include excessive generalization, rigidity, isolation of beliefs, and strong convictions about their truthfulness.[12]

If I Can't Connect, I'll Control

I'll say it again: The greater the threat to our emotional (or physical) selves, the more fearful we become. The ego tells us that we are exposed and in danger. As the ego grows, the more we begin to identify with it, and we come to believe it is the real "I" and needs protection at all costs. Fear of disconnection, then, becomes an existential threat. Our very life is at stake.

Control is the surrogate for connection. To the degree we lack self-esteem, the ego engages to control. It has the dual goal of avoiding vulnerability, which is necessary for connection (hence rendering connection an impossible strategy), and forcing connection through control (which is equally unviable).[13] This is how self-esteem and self-control are intertwined. Self-control leads to the capacity for actual connection—via self-esteem and a reduction of ego—and a genuine sense of autonomy, which is needed for connection. If there is no free, independent self, then there can be no connection to anyone else.

As our self-esteem declines, our capacity to give and receive becomes limited, and the ego engages and moves into "taking mode." The less self-control we have, the more desperately we manipulate events and people around us, especially those closest to us—either overtly or passive-aggressively. Low self-esteem can thus trigger a powerful unconscious desire to usurp authority, overstep bounds, and mistreat those who care about us. When we don't like who we are, we cannot help but become angry with ourselves. Then we take it out on the world around us and on those who care most about us.

Games, Masks, and Hiding Spots

To the degree that we cannot be vulnerable, we seek to control the narrative. We tell and sell the story of who we are and why we exist through the arc of our lives and interactions and must calculate and interpret events to compensate for perceived or genuine faults and flaws.[14] The mask one wears is not so much a disguise as a self-portrait. The eminent psychologist Alfred Adler—who coined the term *inferiority complex*—explains that the psyche's attempt to compensate for our insecurities often shapes the entirety of our lives. We may not even realize how much of our attitudes and behaviors—indeed, our values and beliefs—we style to avoid self-reflection, compensate for self-hatred, and project an image that betrays neither.

We hide our true selves to feel safe. Being authentic—true to who we are—makes us vulnerable and exposes us to the risk of rejection.[15] The fear of this pain drives the real "I" deeper into hiding until we exist only to protect our image. This includes all the games we play and masks we wear to provide the rest of the world with what we believe is the "right" persona, the one that will make us worthy of being loved. The ego's mandate is to avoid the pain of rejection, of feeling less, at all costs.

Although feelings of low self-worth (and accompanying vulnerability) force us into hiding, we don't all hide in the same place. Submissive types become barely visible and hide out of sight—twisting and contorting who they are in a desperate but futile attempt to obtain and maintain connection. They morph into whomever they need to be to avoid confrontation and sidestep rejection. (*If I do whatever you want, then you have to love me.*) Their identity is shackled around the need for acceptance, and they become the quintessential people pleaser. They will blend into the background and become emotionally absent to "not make any waves" and avoid risking disconnection. They go along to get along. This personality type is prone to suffering from an affective disorder.

The dominant type moves into the spotlight, hiding in plain sight.[16] They seek money, power, fame—illusions of worthiness—so that they will become more valuable and deserving of connection, although they settle for fear and awe and assure themselves that they are adored from afar. They will become assertive and aggressive, seeking to control so that they are not controlled, pushing into other people's boundaries to legislate a relationship, to force a connection. Again, all of this is a surrogate for love and acceptance.[17] This personality type is prone to suffering from a personality disorder.

In the extreme, either of these two types may choose isolation, becoming physically absent, to maintain the illusion of control and avoid the threat of rejection altogether. They proactively disconnect to avoid the fear of disconnection. If they are not reliant, then they can never be vulnerable and exposed to being hurt. They live lives of isolation and desperation. Any type of conformity or pressure, whether to time, schedule, or in some cases, social graces, is scorned.

What personality disorders have in common is much greater than what separates them from one another. Although an individual's personality dictates how he deals with feelings of vulnerability and insecurity, the core of egocentricity remains. Just as ice, water, and steam are different states of identical molecules, diverse pathologies are different states of the same agenda. No matter how maladjusted, anyone who suffers from a personality disorder craves connection. Driven by an underlying sense of inferiority, and thus believing themselves to be unworthy of relationships, the ego exerts control in an attempt to establish connection.[18]

Those who suffer from narcissistic personality disorder seek out money, power, and status to make them feel valuable and worthy of connection. The pathology of borderline personality manifests as a need for constant reassurance. With a deep fear of abandonment, they become clingy, absorbed in the lives of others to an unhealthy degree simply to maintain connection. They may also quickly disconnect with rage—to cause pain or avoid pain—if they feel the other person is pulling away. Histrionic personalities adopt tactics similar to their narcissistic counterparts, evoking attention, sympathy, pity, or even anger and disgust. If they have your attention, they have the connection they crave.

We all have an ego, so to some extent we all are disordered. However, as the ego grows more demanding, so does the liklihood of someone developing a personality disorder. As we have seen, disorders are easy to identify if you know what to pay attention to, except for the most dangerous one: sociopathy.

CHAPTER 17

Unmasking Personality Disorders

The terms *sociopath* and *psychopath* are often used interchangeably, in part because of a lack of consensus within the psychiatric community regarding both their origins and their signs and symptoms. What is clear is that the psychopath's autonomic nervous system (which houses the sympathetic nervous system and the fight-flight-freeze response) is wired differently. By contrast, the sociopath, though their condition may have a genetic component, is considered a product of conditioning. Sociopaths were not born that way; they became who they are. Both terms are clinically classified as an antisocial personality disorder, and, for a variety of reasons, we will use *sociopath* to indicate both types.[1]

The sociopath is not psychotic. They know right from wrong but couldn't care less.[2] What is right is always what is in their own best interest, and they believe their actions are completely justified. Sociopaths, therefore, feel zero remorse, no matter who is hurt or harmed. They see reality through the lens of their omnipotent ego. People are objects. Things. There is nothing outside of themselves. Everyone and everything else is irrelevant. Sociopaths move without anxiety because they live without fear of disconnection. They seek domination and control not as a means to connect but as an end unto itself.

For many people, the first step to spotting a sociopath is the most difficult: to accept that people without a conscience exist. It is unsettling to believe that such people walk among us, but it is dangerous to ignore it.

Illuminating Hidden Signs

Not all sociopaths are disciplined; some lack impulse control and suffer from a range of addictive and self-destructive behaviors and habits. The ones who are able to delay gratification and play the long game are the most dangerous because they are meticulous and polished. The sophisticated sociopath often makes an exceptionally good first impression and comes across as warm, empathetic, even altruistic. In *The Mask of Sanity*, Dr. Hervey Cleckley writes that outwardly a sociopath shows nothing that is "brittle or strange," and "everything about him is likely to suggest desirable and superior human qualities, a robust mental health."[3] The diagnostic features of the sociopath, such as superficial charm, lack of remorse or shame, pathological lying, manipulative behavior, and promiscuous behavior, are well known. They are also well hidden—often, until it is too late.

Sociopaths' personalities are carefully crafted to engage and enchant in order to bond and manipulate. Because they are incapable of genuine connection, they become a master at developing interpersonal skills—to don whatever mask they need and play whatever game is required in the moment—to delight and charm an audience of many or of one.

The Extreme Oversell

Such people do not feel guilt or shame. Although they don't relish the consequences of getting caught, losing control, or being exposed, they tend to either believe everything they say or feel perfectly justified in saying it, *even if it is a lie*. Therefore, it isn't possible to detect physiological responses of deception in a sociopath, even with a polygraph test. Their fight-flight-freeze response is offline.[4] They will not show an increase in blood pressure, pulse rate, or galvanic skin response (think sweaty palms) if they do not feel nervous. But there are areas where the sociopath gets tripped up time and again.

A sociopath often does a shockingly awful job of managing the impression they create because they have no real sense of self. They're already wearing a mask every day, so it's as if they're wearing a mask over a mask. When they lie, for instance, they end up sounding like a caricature of an honest person rather than a genuinely honest person. Remember that you shouldn't have to sell the truth. A sociopath will sound like a broken record and will use oversell phrases ad nauseam, as well as trite expressions and age-old clichés, as the centerpiece of their argument or account (see chapter 7 for more).

Because the person is practiced at putting on a show, at presenting an image, they are playing the part of a sincere person to a T. But predictably, they also overshoot their mark. Take eye contact, for example. They routinely make extreme, uncomfortable eye contact because we all know that people who lie look away, and they're going to show you just how truthful they are. Therefore, their gaze often extends well beyond the comfort zone—until the point where you feel like squirming. This person's gaze is often intensely penetrating, lasting much longer than that of an emotionally healthy person who is honestly expressing themselves.

Another giveaway is the display of faux vulnerability. They may put their "great humility" on display by making themselves seem meek and unassuming. The unskilled observer may believe that this is the sociopath unmasked. It is yet another mask.[5] Genuine humility is a powerful tool to connection, and here's why: A person strides into the room, head held high, faint smile, shoulders back, breezing with confidence. A turn-on? Not so much. Whether it's a fleeting interaction or a long-term relationship, if someone is self-absorbed, they do not build connection with anyone else. This is why we are repelled by arrogant people and attracted to those who are humble. The time-honored centerpiece of charisma-enhancement advice is to try to appear as confident as you can—to look impressive. But that conventional wisdom is incorrect. Confidence without humility equals arrogance—and is a huge *turnoff*. Nobody likes people who are full of themselves, and the sociopath knows this all too well. Human beings are innately attracted to humility, which is the mark of actual self-esteem.

higher self-esteem $\rightarrow$ smaller ego $\rightarrow$ humility $\rightarrow$ connection

lower self-esteem $\rightarrow$ increased ego $\rightarrow$ arrogance $\rightarrow$ disconnection

Illuminating one's own fallibility shows authenticity and trust—two traits that provide for an acclerated connection. Again, the tip-off is that the sociopath goes overboard. They cannot calibrate their impression management. They're like an actor who works hard to figure out how to represent a charming and interested character. They may stand meekly, let drop a few selected insecurities, or display over-the-top interest in, deference to, or reverence for you. As intoxicating as this may be for our ego, you'll recall from chapter 9 how easily flattery corrupts our judgment.[6]

The polished sociopath will regale others with his love for all things human—just causes and moral pursuits.[7] His sterling character is on full display. His fatal flaw, again, is that he oversells and underdelivers. And when he thinks no one is watching, he never delivers. If you pay attention, you will note strong incongruencies between what he says and what he does.

The above indications may prove helpful, but they are hardly definitive. It would be incorrect to say that emotionally healthy and honest people will never make extreme eye contact or try their hardest to convince you of something that they genuinely believe; and certainly, the signs of humility and its counterfeit are easy to conflate and confuse.

A Peek behind the Mask

Sociopaths shy away from situations or topics that may trigger uncontrollable feelings—particularly fear. In conversation, topics of childhood difficulties or unrequited love will be absent. Should the subject unexpectedly hit an emotional vein, they might express incongruent emotions (e.g., giggle wildly when talking about being hungry and homeless as a child), a function of a last-ditch ego-defense mechanism. We draw a contrast with one who may use humor as a defense mechanism and one who, with perspective, will offer a wry observation. As Mark Twain once quipped, "Comedy is tragedy plus time." Because of their need to feel omnipotent (which contrasts with the inherent nature of dependence), a sociopath will rarely speak about their emotional or social needs. They will, however, talk freely about a desire for money, power, and control, as well as biological necessities, such as food and clothing.

> In their element and in control, the sociopath wears a facade that is inscrutable and impenetrable. Their actions and interactions reveal nothing of their real self. But knock them off balance, and instead of a measured response, you might just get a genuine reaction—a glimpse into what lies behind the mask.

In their element and in control, the sociopath wears a facade that is inscrutable and impenetrable. Their actions and interactions reveal nothing of their real self. But knock them off balance, and instead of a measured response, you might just get a genuine reaction—a glimpse into what lies behind the mask. We observe, then, how they navigate the waters of vulnerability in situations where they have lost control.

Up against the Wall

The sociopath—or someone with another personality disorder with sociopathic features—knows how to push the right psychological buttons to gain control in a relationship. Once they have achieved a degree of compliance, they will seek to undermine their target's emotional stability. This is why they love to be unpredictable. (Most personality disorders have this in common.) Sometimes their behavior—such as running hot and cold—is due to the particular disorder; other times, it is purely tactical.[8]

The more off balance you are, the more in control they become. Their intent is to undermine your safety and security, both within yourself and in your relationship with them. They want you to feel unsure and insecure. They know that the less assured you are, the more willing you are to put up with them (in general) or to comply with their immediate requests. This is because our need for connection remains; the more fearful we are of losing that connection, the more power they hold over us. The keys to you feeling accepted, safe, and secure are in their pocket.

Their posture may become aggressive. Alternatively, they may scream without saying a word, by shutting down. They inflict pain. You'll fear their disconnection as they attack your insecurities with radio silence. While seemingly paradoxical, giving in provides us with a feeling of control. When we allow ourselves to be controlled, the situation and the other person's behavior follow a familiar trajectory that ensures a predictable outcome. The thought *What will happen next?* is too overwhelming. The ego must take the path of least resistance to avert the greatest disaster—the unknown.

All-Out War

A sociopath's worst tendencies quickly surface when they feel that they are losing control over you. When they find that you are not "obedient," they will move predictably into full-out attack mode. Say goodbye to the veneer of civility. They'll hurl every accusation at you and about you to anyone who will listen—friends, neighbors, coworkers. They'll use their gift of the gab to weave fanciful tales about you and your wrongs. They will lie. They'll fabricate stories to destroy your reputation. They'll win the court of public opinion, turn people against you, and attack you by proxy.

They are all too eager to take you to court because, to them, the name of the game is power. The more they can keep you on edge, the more control they feel. In court, they file endless motions and make baseless claims to sap your strength. They are *energized* by conflict. Mediation or arbitration is always a waste of time because they have no interest in being even remotely reasonable. They won't give ground. Any indication that they are doing so is likely a tactic to buy more time—and to drain you emotionally, physically, and financially.

Regardless of one's personality or accompanying disorder, our emotional well-being is inextricably linked with the quality of the relationships we have. Research confirms what we know to be true: The ability to form and maintain good relationships is central to our mental health.[9] In the domain of relationships, a person—even a sociopath—can't help but give themselves away. Best of all, you're about to see that there's much to watch out for, well before it's too late.

CHAPTER 18

Reflections of Relationships

The people we know who are emotionally healthy enjoy generally positive relationships. Conversely, those who don't seem to get along with anyone likely have a host of emotional issues. Much unhappiness in life stems from failing or failed relationships, with our emotional health feasting on, and fueling, the quality of our relationships. William Glasser, noted psychiatrist and founder of reality therapy, writes:

> From the perspective of forty years of psychiatric practice, it has become apparent to me that all unhappy people have the same problem: they are unable to get along with the people they want to get along well with.[1]

Letting others into our emotional space and entering theirs requires a diminution of the "I." When the wall of "I am me and he is he" is broken down, there is connection, a bond. To be a part of someone's life, we need to create space for that person. If one is too self-absorbed, there is no room for anyone else. Our capacity to give love and to receive love is strained, if not altogether severed.[2]

Those who are in emotional pain become more absorbed in

themselves. This is similar to physical pain, whereby someone with a toothache, for instance, finds it difficult to focus on the needs of another. The typical characteristics of the egocentric mentality are arrogance and bravado, but even a submissive personality who is seemingly void of ego can also be self-centered and selfish. He is consumed by his own pain, filled with self-pity, and unable to feel anyone else's pain while drowning in his own.[3] Such a person experiences no real connection to anyone outside of himself, despite his seemingly noble nature. He will not—cannot—burden himself unless he receives a larger payout in the form of acceptance or approval. His taking is disguised as giving. His fear is dressed up as love. (He may also be motivated by the need to assuage feelings of guilt or inadequacy, yet still his aim is to reduce his own suffering, not someone else's.)

The more self-esteem we have, the more complete we are. Receiving, after all, is a natural and reciprocal consequence of giving. The cycle of giving and receiving is the perfect union. In fact, research has even shown that certain areas of the brain exhibit elevated levels of activity when a person gives. Giving literally excites the brain.[4] When we only take, however, we are left feeling empty and are forced to take repeatedly in a futile attempt to feel complete. Constant taking only reinforces our dependency and continues to exhaust us and others.

Every positive emotion stems from giving and flows outward from us to others, while every negative emotion revolves around taking. Do not confuse lust for love. When we lust after someone or something, we think in terms of what they (or it) can do for us. When we love, however, our thoughts are immersed in what we can give to someone else. Giving makes us feel good, so we do it happily. But when we lust, we want only to take. When someone we love is in pain, we feel pain. When someone whom we lust for is in pain, we think only in terms of what that loss or inconvenience means to us.

Eliminating False Positives

Having colored in more of the psychological picture, you will find it easier to detect low self-esteem in a person by the way he speaks and behaves. Still, the potential for miscues abound. For example, a person who "gives" to be liked can often, at first glance, be confused with one who is giving because it is the right thing to do or because they want to give. The same action will cause two distinct emotional imprints, based on their intention. It is the difference between giving a donation and being mugged. In both cases, money is going from one person to another, but one instance is empowering, while the other is weakening. Accordingly, one act enhances self-esteem, while the other is emotionally draining. If you give out of fear or guilt, your self-esteem is not enriched; indeed, it is only diminished. You aren't really giving; the other person is taking. You are being taken advantage of, with your consent.

Suppose you notice that someone habitually acquiesces to the wishes of others. Is this because he genuinely wishes to be helpful or because he's afraid to say no or does not feel worthy of asserting his feelings? Solely observing his gracious behavior, we cannot distinguish between a person who is humble and enjoys high self-esteem and one who allows himself to become a doormat.[5] Likewise, we can't presume that someone who gives in to make peace has low self-esteem and needs to avoid confrontation or that he recognizes what matters and moves his ego out of the way. At the same time, holding one's ground may signal obstinance and defiance, an indication of extreme arrogance—*I'm never wrong; it's always the other guy*—which, in turn, stems from low self-esteem. Perhaps, however, not acquiescing suggests that someone is choosing to enforce proper boundaries and not allowing himself to be manipulated by a person who is trying to play on his emotions.

How does the trait of humility—the seed of self-esteem—translate into observable signs, particularly when someone's behavior may be nearly indistinguishable from the opposite?

The Impression of Relationships

The image below demonstrates negative space. Focus on the white image and we see a vase; focus on the black space and we see two profiles facing each other. Each space, positive and negative, defines the other.

Self-esteem is keenly observed as a reflection of one's relationships and manifests in three main domains: one's history and patterns, interactions and exchanges, and borders and boundaries.

History and Patterns

"Intelligence is the ability to learn from your mistakes," the saying goes. "Wisdom is the ability to learn from the mistakes of others." Observe the quality of someone's relationships and how he speaks about people in his life—both past and present. Does he have several good friends who have been in his life for a number of years, or a few short-term or fleeting friendships? How does he talk about his family? His siblings? His parents? Does he take responsibility for any relationships that have soured, or do they all seem to evaporate into bitter disappointment and resentment? A word of caution: You must let the evidence speak for itself rather than rely on the person's own description of his relationships. Certain individuals are "best friends" with the world and love everyone, and they wrongly assume that everyone loves them in return. Such people have grandiose and flawed perceptions of how they are viewed by others.

In the professional arena, the single best question to ask a candidate is an open-ended question about his last job, boss, and coworkers: "Tell me about things at XYZ Corp." or "Describe your working relationship with your coworkers." Then take note of how he speaks about his previous job, paying close attention to phrases (e.g., "Nobody there understood me"; "They never took my ideas seriously"; "My boss was out to get me"; "I had a personality conflict with my supervisor"). You want to look for someone who assumes a degree of responsibility for his personal success and interpersonal relationships. This doesn't mean that he's not entitled to have mixed feelings and a little ill will, but if someone doesn't have the emotional intelligence to recognize that he is coming across as resentful, hostile, or spiteful, that in itself is a red flag. To this end, beware of any bold, broad, or sweeping statements that speak to incessant frustration (e.g., "Everyone there is out for themselves"; "You wouldn't believe the crazy things going on there"; "Nobody there liked working for our manager"). His perception is cause for concern, and his lack of discretion drips with even greater concern.

Interactions and Exchanges

Someone who lacks self-esteem may indulge in things to satisfy his own desires yet not treat others particularly well. Or he may overly cater to others because he craves their approval and respect, but he does not take care of his own needs. Only a person who truly has self-respect will treat himself *and* others well. And when I say *well*, I don't mean he engages in short-term gratification. Rather, he invests in his long-term well-being and is kind and good to others—not so they will like him but because it is the right thing to do.

Here we are especially interested in how someone treats those he

In the professional arena, the single best question to ask a candidate is an open-ended question about his last job, boss, and coworkers. . . . You want to look for someone who assumes a degree of responsibility for his personal success and interpersonal relationships. This doesn't mean that he's not entitled to have mixed feelings and a little ill will, but if someone doesn't have the emotional intelligence to recognize that he is coming across as resentful, hostile, or spiteful, that in itself is a red flag.

"doesn't have to be nice to" and "doesn't need to impress," such as the waiter, receptionist, or doorman. You will also want to note how he treats those who will not likely turn away from him, no matter how foul his behavior, such as an employee or dependent family member.

Be on alert for the two-faced person with an inconsistent personality. He might be nice to us but not so polite to others. Of course, if he treats us poorly but others well, we already know we've got a problem. Yet the former is also a concern because it indicates that he's adjusting his conduct toward us for his own gain; his behavior toward us does not reflect his true self.

A person who respects himself is capable of respecting others and thus conducts himself with integrity. Does he make commitments and stick to them—whether it is keeping an appointment or helping a friend in need? Or does something always seem to come up that interferes with him being able to follow through? Is he a person of his word, and can he be trusted? When he borrows something, does he return it in good shape and without delay? Or do you constantly have to chase him down to repay a debt or an obligation? Is he careful about the truth, even when it comes at his own expense? Or does he tell lies that advance his personal agenda or take advantage of others?[6]

Borders and Boundaries

A poor self-image often translates into porous borders—because if a person does not have a clear definition of himself, he is unable to recognize what is proper between himself and another. This may manifest as a chronically needy person who asks to be rescued from every self-made crisis or as a controlling personality who pushes his way into other peoples' space.

Healthy boundaries are not created to keep people out but rather to define our space and our sense of personal responsibility. Does this person have a clear sense of appropriate behavior, given the relationship? Does she make unreasonable requests of people she has just met or barely knows? Does she believe in reciprocating, or does she prefer to do the taking?

We should ask ourselves if she respects or violates rules and the rights of others. For instance, we say, "I'm on a diet, please don't bring cake," but she brings it anyway, because she can't show up empty-handed. He says he can fix our computer, and even though we tell him not to, he takes it anyway because he wants to surprise us by fixing it. Minor infractions? Perhaps, but perhaps not. The presence or absence of a pattern answers this question. As we learned with our accident-prone cadet in chapter 4, it is a red flag whenever an individual frequently interacts inconsistently with their status in a given dynamic.

Depending on the nature of the relationship, the boundary violator turns on the psychological pressure and stokes our latent insecurities. The more you question yourself, the less you'll question him. This is one of his favorite tactics.

People inherently need to perform in a manner consistent with how they see themselves and how they think others perceive them. The person who seeks to coerce others may apply this psychology by incorporating themes such as friendship, family, partnership, commitment to work, a sense of decency—all qualities that most people aspire to identify with. A question such as "Isn't it amazing how some people don't know the definition of the word *family* or *loyalty?*" is so powerful. When it comes to some people (perhaps even ourselves), we may be particularly vulnerable because (a) we need to think of ourselves as good and noble, and more susceptible to the opinions of others, and (b) we have a greater need for internal consistency. To reduce uncertainty, we prefer to see others, the world, and most certainly ourselves as predictable and stable.

The manipulator's ace in the hole is to make you feel ashamed that you're not coming to their aid. They remind you of how *bad* you really are. They'll be convincing, too (because part of you believes they're right). The threat of disconnection creates fear, and they try yet again to circumvent your logical defenses. You become frantic to extinguish those glowing embers of shame, which is accomplished only by "doing right by them." For the same reason that some people (perhaps you) cannot easily *say* no—for fear of rejection—this person cannot *hear* no, because it is internalized as rejection, which reinforces their own deep-seated fear of unworthiness.

Although an unrelenting pattern of these behaviors points to a personality disorder, we should remind ourselves yet again that, at times, even the healthiest among us may resort to these tactics. The person may be in legitimate pain. Manipulation isn't always conscious. Yet even when his manipulation is conscious, there may still be a good reason for you to say yes. Here's an example: Suppose your elderly aunt wants you to visit and talks about how she is getting up in years, and who knows how long she'll be around. It's the kind of loving guilt trip that only family can lay on you. But just because you can see through your aunt's attempt at persuasion doesn't mean you should abandon your conscience or responsibilities.

Other boundary violations include:

- Making improper remarks or asking embarrassing or highly personal questions of someone he barely knows without at least a casual, perfunctory preface or sincere regret afterward

- Being oblivious to social cues and violating others' personal space. This person is unable to read people's responses to his behavior (e.g., if he is too loud and others show noticeable signs of discomfort, but he does not pick up on it; if he stands too close while talking).
- Being sexually seductive or overly flirtatious or familiar with someone he just met or barely knows (e.g., calls a doctor he sees for the first time by his first name and pats him on the back; hugs people who don't even know him)
- Not hearing *no*, being really pushy, or forcing his opinion on others (e.g., offers to do something, and ignores the word *no*, even when it is said numerous times; ignores someone's clear indication that they are uncomfortable with doing something; ignores someone else's opinion and pushes his own opinion on them; he shows no regard for others' wishes).
- Neglecting social norms and universal boundaries. Does this person have respect for law and order, structure and civility, or does he disregard social norms and feel that laws and rules do not apply to him?

Be sure to filter out false positives. Emotionally healthy people are able to solicit help, when appropriate, rather than let a sense of pride or embarrassment—a function of the ego—stand in the way. A person who tells you not to call a doctor or an ambulance when he experiences chest pains because he "doesn't want anyone to make a big fuss over him" is not operating with optimum mental health. This is the kind of person who freely drops his pennies into the "Take a penny, leave a penny" container but finds it difficult to *take* a penny. He may say yes to the endless demands of others, but won't ask someone else for the smallest of favors.

An individual with proper boundaries is willing and able to offer to help others when such help is reasonable. And at the same time, he can ask others for help in a responsible, direct, and nonmanipulative manner.

The healthier our relationships, the healthier we are, and the more we are able to move responsibly toward our life's purpose without the need for ego-oriented approval and without surrendering to the blinding fix of immediate gratification. Likewise, the happier we are with the direction and pace of our lives, the less frustrated we are with ourselves and the more tolerant and patient we become with others. The more we give in to ourselves, the more we demand that the world accommodate us, which sets the stage for unhealthy interactions and relationships. But as I have noted throughout the book, personality directs pathology. Not everyone makes *their* problem *your* problem. In the next chapter, we will learn how to fine-tune our read of those who may be suffering silently on the inside.

CHAPTER 19

Highs and Lows and
Suffering in Between

A narrow perspective means a shrinking world and an expanding "I." The frequent use of personal pronouns (e.g., *I, me*) defines the egocentric experience because emotional distress orients a person's attention inward. As expected, those suffering from anxiety or depression use personal pronouns at a higher rate.[1] They also speak with greater verbal immediacy, using present tense verbs, which indicates a lack of perspective or psychological distance.[2] When they are under a modicum of stress, their language has a defeatist tinge (e.g., using words such as *overwhelmed, deluged,* and *crushed*). Their mindset is not of overcoming but of being overcome (e.g., "I can't take anymore"; "I'm losing it"; "I'm falling apart").

Reliable indicators of the depressive self-focusing style include emphasis on negative over positive stimuli and rumination on negative thoughts and fears.[3] Even an insignificant event puts their fertile imagination into overdrive, consuming them with mushrooming fears and anxieties. Their lives become filled with "never-ending tragedies" that never actually happen.

The Focusing Illusion

The inability to let go of worrisome and pervasive thoughts spirals their mood further downward.[4] They bring their distress to life by giving a negative thought or impulse more attention than it deserves, fueling it with the energy it needs to sustain itself.

Daniel Kahneman, who coined the term *focusing illusion*, explains that nothing is as important as you think it is when you're thinking about it.[5] To a large extent, when we redirect our focus, it loses its pull. When our perspective is narrow, we cannot do this, and we lose control of our thoughts, allowing them to become all-consuming. The spiral reinforces itself.[6] Our time and energy elevate the significance of the thoughts. Our mind logically concludes, *This must be important because why else would I spend all of this time thinking about it?* For instance, someone with several job offers is likely to see and evaluate each offer with objective diligence. However, when a person has been unemployed for two years, has a stack of bills on his kitchen table, and finally lands a job interview, his perspective is different, narrowed. His thoughts become all-consuming. He will repeatedly go over the interview in his mind, think about it nonstop, and obsess over every minute detail—all the while fearing he won't get the job. In fact, he expects he won't get the job.

The ego is preferentially oriented to dwell on the worst-case scenario to protect itself from unpleasant surprises. Here's the psychology in play: If someone rear-ends your car, you might understandably feel shaken and angry. But if you knew in the morning that this would happen later in the day, when the moment came, you would feel jarred but much less surprised and thus experience little or no fear. This is critical to understand: Fear exists because of a loss of control. Something happens that was not only undesirable but also unanticipated. In the same way that the ego seeks to control others and circumstances, it adjusts our expectations—and leads us to expect the worst—and we automatically eliminate the element of surprise in any given situation. Thus, we reduce our shock and feeling of being out of control because we predicted it. We get to be right. Fulfilled expectations provide a layer of perverted relief.

This presents a real one-two punch. The ego focuses on the negative, and the attention itself assigns greater importance to the object of our focus, magnifying its significance, which then reinforces the need to pay greater attention. We then spiral into an increasingly narrow perspective and emotional instability. It only makes sense that our mood sours and swings. For those keeping score, the ego corrupts our mindset in five ways: (a) It chooses what we focus on, (b) it makes what we see all about us, (c) it concludes that all negative experiences are due to a deficiency within ourselves, (d) it magnifies the relevance of our focus, and (e) it causes us to believe that we can think our way out of a situation that is beyond our control or understand something that is unknowable.

Feeling Blue but Not to You

We might assume that a person who suffers from an affective disorder will heavily pepper their language with negatively charged adjectives and adverbs (e.g., *down, lonely, lost, sick, sadly, uneasily*). But this is not always the case.[7] People who are feeling anxious or sad, may actually avoid using these words in order to hide their true feelings from others.[8] They moderate the disclosure of negative emotions to avoid alienating others and further isolating themselves.[9] Findings show that only private (e.g., personal journals, anonymous blogs and forums) but not public disclosure of negative emotions through word usage signifies a depressive state.[10] The rich use of positively charged language is, however, inversely correlated with depression in both public and private forums. In other words, it's easier to filter out the negative but harder to use upbeat and optimistic language when we're not feeling it. Public discourse and open conversation are revealing in what is typically missing.

The least depression-oriented topics and language contain not only many positive affect terms (e.g., *lol, haha, love, miss*) but also words related to family activities (e.g., *car, weekend, home, family*) and social activities (e.g., *food, tonight, dog, run, dinner, weather, weekend*).[11]

In open but guarded communication, another linguistic signal flies below the conscious radar: The previously noted use of absolutist language is a better indicator of emotional disturbance than either pronoun type or negative emotion words.[12] The prevalence of absolutist words is approximately 50 percent greater in anxiety and depression forums compared to nineteen different control forums (general interest sites), and it is approximately 80 percent greater for suicidal ideation forums.[13] Absolutist words are also a more accurate predictor of a future depressive relapse.[14]

The Mind-Body Connection

While psychological or emotional problems may be classified under the broad umbrella of mental health disorders, they are directly correlated with our physical health. Psychological disorders typically present with both psychological (mind and emotions) and somatic (biological and physiological) symptoms. For example, people who suffer from clinical depression often exhibit bodily symptoms such as vague aches and pains, insomnia, fatigue, energy loss, gastrointestinal problems, appetite changes, chronic joint pain, significant weight gain or loss, and psychomotor changes (e.g., slower motor movements or speeded-up, agitated movements). Those who suffer from an emotional disorder are prone to suffer more physical pain for myriad reasons.

The inability to foster healthy connections exacerbates emotional—and oftentimes physical—isolation. Feeling alone or experiencing loneliness, more than any other factor, causes extreme stress and an overall weakening of the immune system. Functional magnetic resonance imaging (fMRI) scans reveal that two areas of the brain where you process physical pain—the *dorsal anterior cingulate cortex* and the *anterior insula*—become activated when you experience feelings of isolation.[15] This explains why major depression is associated with a decreased pain threshold.[16]

Feelings of hopelessness and "giving up" trigger the autonomic nervous system and the pituitary-adrenal cortical system, which impairs the immune system and produces a cascading disruption of our physiology and bodily functions.[17] Constant anxiety causes an endorphin discharge. Endorphins are endogenous morphines produced by the body to regulate pain by decreasing the amount of pain transmitter taken up by neurons in the brain. More endorphins mean fewer pain impulses.[18] Moreover, persistent anxiety moves us into the fight-flight-freeze zone, and the subsequent cortisol and adrenaline levels can have a devastating effect on our organs and bodily functions.

Driver or Passenger

The frequent use of the personal pronoun *me* indicates self-focus, but unlike the pronoun *I*, it almost always is used in a passive tense and may be indicative of passive tendencies or feelings of helplessness and vulnerability.[19] Some people do not suffer so silently. When the veneer of pretense loses its luster, the pain comes through, unfiltered.[20] We hear all about "me."

Passivity manifests in complaining and blaming because these behaviors are both self-focused and correlate to feelings of helplessness. These people are likely to make frequent complaints with the accompanying message that no one will do anything about them and make demands to mobilize feelings of guilt and responsibility in those around them.[21] Their pain is, they tell you, the result of someone or something else outside of themselves (e.g., "You make me sad"; "All this noise makes me feel anxious"). This is not to say that a correlation does not exist, but a complete lack of ownership over one's emotional state points to a mood disorder because, quite logically, if how we feel is directly determined by an external cause, then we, too, would become anxious and ultimately depressed.

Dr. William Glasser writes, "To be depressed or neurotic is passive. It happened to us; we are its victim, and we have no control over it."[22] Linguists consider a sentence to be illogical if it is semantically incorrect. Consider the statement "My friend forced me to have blue eyes." No one would accept this sentence as truthful. However, we easily accept the declaration "My friend makes me angry." Both statements, though, are semantically identical and, according to linguists, structurally incorrect.

> When the first person, the one doing the causing, is different from the person experiencing the anger, the sentence is said to be semantically ill-formed and unacceptable. The semantic ill-formedness of sentences of this type arises because it, literally, is not possible for one human being to create an emotion in another human being—thus, we reject sentences of this form. Therefore, sentences of this type identify a model in which the person assigns responsibility for his emotions to people or forces outside his control. The act itself does not cause the emotion; rather, the emotion is a response generated from a model in which the person takes no responsibility for experiences which he could control.[23]

When we assign responsibility for our emotions to people or forces outside of our control, we become an object or an effect of the experience rather than the cause. The themes of agency (a sense of control over one's life) and communion (a feeling of connectedness with others) continue to play out over and again. Remember that a lack of self-control inhibits connection, and the ego engages to control others and compel connection. The equation comes back to our ability to be responsible: Self-control leads to self-esteem and a reduction of the ego and the capacity to connect with others; it makes communion possible. Feeling ineffective in our lives—helpless and hopeless to effect a positive change—unsurprisingly coincides with poor emotional health.[24] Research finds that a personal narrative with both agency and communion correlates with positive emotional well-being.[25]

To be emotionally healthy, we need to believe that if we take action X, it can influence result Y. *Learned helplessness,* a term coined by psychologist Martin Seligman, occurs when a person feels that since he is not in control, he might as well give up. Seligman maintains that people have a perception of helplessness when they believe that their actions will not be able to influence their outcomes.[26] The accompanying feeling of futility—that what we do doesn't matter—leads to the inevitable, excruciating conclusion that *we* don't matter.

Multiple experiments show that people who are exposed to unpleasant conditions that they cannot control will afterward become withdrawn. In one such experiment, subjects were exposed to extremely high levels of noise. By pushing a button, one group could stop the noise, while the other could not stop the noise. A short while later, when both groups were brought together, individuals from the group who could do nothing about the noise—who were helpless—showed little interest when asked to participate in a sport or a game and showed little motivation to win.[27]

When someone's sense of agency becomes severely compromised, they abandon the real "I" and resign themselves to victimhood.[28] They believe that everyone else makes the decisions while they are totally subject to external forces, unable to take charge or make change.[29] The person is unable to see themselves as the initiator of experiences; rather, they are subject to the capricious whims of fate and circumstance or are a victim of inexorable desire or a callous society.[30]

The ego is a meaning-making machine. And when it's directing, it will cast itself and its world in whatever role it chooses. Interestingly, it will not always cast itself as the hero and others as villains. It is not uncommon for someone to declare themselves worthless—so damaged, bad, and broken that they are beyond repair or reproach. This unconsciously motivated, ego-driven tactic cleverly recuses them of responsibility because they don't "deserve" to be happy. They thereby avoid the pain of accountability and the burden of obligation. Unable to face the legitimate challenges of life, the ego of this type shrewdly switches tactics and declares itself to be a casualty of fate, circumstance, or others' cruel conniving.

> When we assign responsibility for our emotions to people or forces outside of our control, we become an object or an effect of the experience rather than the cause.

Whatever the narrative, we become locked into these patterns and too often we manipulate events to unfold in accordance with our expectations. It's how we need the world to be. Being right becomes more of an emotional priority than being happy. We align the entirety of our lives to accommodate *our story*.

From Neurosis to Psychosis

What's the difference between neurosis and psychosis? Think of neurosis as anxiety, insecurity, irrational fears. Most of us suffer with neurosis to some degree. People with severe neurotic tendencies have difficulty adapting to and coping with change as well as an inability to develop a rich, complex, satisfying personality. Pronounced neurotic tendencies can manifest as both an affective disorder and a personality disorder. Psychosis is a break with reality.

We have learned that the ego is equipped with an elaborate array of defense mechanisms to effectively deal with life's little (and not so little) bumps. However, when trauma strikes, one's personal narrative requires a fast and bold rewrite.[31] When we cannot integrate a traumatic experience into our narrative, something has to give. Someone suffering from extreme depression may sadly attempt suicide to leave the physical world. Someone suffering from psychosis stays in the physical world but abandons reality.

Psychosis occurs when a person has distorted reality to such a degree that it bears little resemblance to reality. He loses touch with what is real. Think hallucinations. He might hear, smell, and feel things that are not real. He may also have delusions and hold strong beliefs that are not real, such as thinking he is speaking with the president, or that are dark, like believing he is speaking with the devil. (Perhaps in some administrations, these are one in the same.) Persecutory delusions are most common. This means they feel exploited, harassed, controlled, or followed. They may believe their thoughts are being broadcast for all to hear. They might experience thought insertions and believe, "My thoughts are not my own."[32]

Although psychosis is symptomatic of schizophrenia, it is also common in bipolar disorder. These psychotic features can be mood-congruent (consistent what his state) or mood-incongruent (conflicting with his state). In a manic state, mood-congruent feelings of grandiosity may amplify with the belief that one has magical powers or enjoys a special relationship with a famous person. During a depressive episode feelings of guilt, inadequacy, and shame, may expand into hearing voices of condemnation or delusions that they have caused great harm or committed a heinous crime.

When one's emotional health becomes increasingly compromised, these connections become forced constructions of a fragile, insecure, self-loathing ego that has itself at the center of an angry, vengeful universe. A person's assumptions range from the general (e.g., "I hate me, so you must hate me") to the specific (e.g., "I am insecure about the shape of my head, so I see you staring at it, which confirms my beliefs that it is misshapen"). He will "see" what he needs to see, believe what he needs to believe, in order to prove to himself that he is all-knowing and in control. Safe. Secure. He cannot be vulnerable, so he manipulates his worldview until it accommodates his insecurities (in stark contrast to the sociopath, who twists and turns others until they accommodate him).

Even the thoughts, feelings, and intentions of others are "known" to him, absent logical grounds and even with evidence to the contrary (e.g., "I know you are annoyed with me"; "I feel that you're curious about what's happening"). Ironically, the less healthy a person is, the more he believes in his ability to see, know, and predict the world around him. In actuality, he is less able to recognize cause-and-effect relationships. To compensate for his impairment, he creates his own associations between action and consequence. Naturally, this compounds his illness because, when the inevitable breach occurs, he retreats deeper into his assumptions.

Superstition is nothing but a diluted form of psychosis—the desire to make connections where none exist. Superstition sets in when the relationship between cause and effect is blurred. This can make us virtual slaves to rituals and compulsive behaviors. We need to feel some sense of control, so we draw our own association between an event and a behavior. If we knock three times, for example, then the meeting will go well. These types of behavior give us a feeling of empowerment. Reality is supplanted by the ego's own self-oriented correlations. Since a person cannot find meaning or significance, he invents it.

The Language Markers

At times, even the healthiest among us becomes frazzled, overwhelmed, or otherwise distracted and unable to speak calmly and clearly. It's no reason for alarm. However, a pattern of short, simple sentences that lack cohesion—a clear connection from one point to the next—can indicate the presence or onset of psychosis.

Using computer analysis of speech patterns, researchers have been able to not only diagnose psychosis but also predict with an astounding 100 percent accuracy those who would go on to experience a psychotic episode. There are two markers: (a) a disjointed narrative (lacking clear flow and cogency) and (b) a shorter, less complex sentence structure, which produces a starburst-like speech pattern.[33] This was evident by a poor use of relative pronouns (e.g., *that* or *which* to introduce dependent clauses), which frequently did not clearly indicate who or what was previously described and caused decreased referential cohesion.[34] An individual suffering from psychosis believes their perspective is universally shared. The aberrant ego constructs its own

> A pattern of short, simple sentences that lack cohesion—a clear connection from one point to the next—can indicate the presence or onset of psychosis.

reality, making contrived connections and assumptions of a shared knowledge base. Meeting someone for the first time, this person will speak as if the other person should know what they are talking about.

Such people also don't have a firm grasp of temporal or spatial relationships. A lack of contextual language, including relative words such as *yesterday, lately,* and *nearby,* is thus predictive of the severity of the psychosis.[35] Regardless of pathology and diagnosis, the following visual cues indicate the presence of mental health issues, and when observed, they should receive close attention:[36]

- Seems very distracted (can't focus, looks around; responds to or notices every movement or noise); very fidgety; can't sit still (e.g., constantly moves, shakes leg, or picks lint off clothing)
- Displays odd or highly idiosyncratic behaviors (e.g., constantly straightens things for no obvious purpose; avoids

stepping on cracks; makes odd, repetitive movements); has peculiar speech (e.g., speaks in a monotone voice with no vocal inflection); posture and/or gait are stiff, rigid, very awkward.

- Appears detached or cold (e.g., very unfriendly; perhaps somewhat rude, aloof—reluctant to interact but in an un-friendly, rather than shy, manner; does not respond in a warm or friendly manner to others' kindness or friendliness)
- Acts paranoid or suspicious (e.g., is untrusting; eyes may dart, looks around constantly; may refuse to shake your hand, as if you intend to harm him in some way; appears overly guarded)
- Exhibits poor hygiene or unkempt appearance (e.g., is un-shaven and appears not to have showered in a few days; hair looks messy and dirty; clothes are rumpled or dirty)

A mentally ill person is not necessarily violent or dangerous. In actuality, most acts of violence are committed by individuals who are not suffering from mental illness. But this doesn't mean that there are not clear and definitive warning signs. Building on your observation skills, the final chapter will help you gauge whether a person is likely to pose a threat to your safety and well-being.

CHAPTER 20

When to Worry:
Red Alert and Warning Signs

When it comes to investments, we are reminded that "past performance may not be indicative of future results," but with people, you can expect that past performance may well indicate future results. In his book *Inside the Criminal Mind,* noted criminologist Stanton Samenow explains, "It is impossible to commit a crime that is out of character. It would be like asking a building to fly; it is not within the building's nature to do so."[1] He expounds that even the perpetrator who commits a "crime of passion"—where he appears to lose control and commits a single, unplanned crime—has much in common with the calculating cold-blooded murderer. He writes:

> Blustery, inflexible, and impatient, each demand that others do what he wants. They may flare up at even minor slights. Instead of coping constructively with unpleasant situations, they compound their problems. When frustrated or disappointed they blame others. . . . The "out of character" crime may be preceded by a long series of threats or assaults that were hushed up or disregarded by the family. Despite appearances, when the homicide is finally committed, it is by a person to whom violence is no stranger.[2]

People don't just snap. There are almost always identifiable behaviors that will allow you to know when violence may be looming. To start, ask yourself the following questions about your subject:

- When angered, does he lash out at inanimate objects— punching walls, throwing objects—or engage in symbolic destruction, such as ripping photos, destroying documents, or throwing his wedding ring?
- Does she tend to make threats or use violence in an attempt to resolve conflict or to get her way?
- Does he overreact to little things and assume others have a personal motive for crossing him? For instance, if the secretary gives him the wrong information or someone relays poor instructions, does he become enraged, believing their motivation was intentional and personal?
- Is she cruel to animals or, for that matter, to people? Does she say hurtful things or seek to embarrass or humiliate others, particularly those who cannot easily defend themselves?
- Has he not moved up the corporate ladder, and does he show frustration with his lack of progress? Does he feel that no one appreciates his contributions or feel that others take credit for his work and that everyone is out to get him?
- Has there been a sudden decline in her attitude, performance, or behavior? Does she suddenly seem disinterested and unaffected by the goings-on at work or at home?

Although these indications will give you advanced warning for any pending concerns, do not underestimate the role of drugs and alcohol. Research finds that 31 percent of people who had both a substance abuse disorder and a psychiatric disorder committed at least one act of violence in a year, compared with 18 percent of people with a psychiatric disorder alone.[3] Likewise, being a young male or a substance abuser puts you at a greater risk for violent behavior than being mentally ill—and combining the risk factors points to an even greater statistical propensity.[4] Beyond this, if someone talks at all about being "fed up" or "sick and tired" of "everyone and everything" or generally about a plan to get even or solve his problems, be alert. Of course, you should be extra vigilant if he has detailed plans to commit acts of violence, speaks about settling debts or getting respect, and has easy access to a weapon. Other troubling indicators include if he even jokes or comments about weapons or settling the score, displays pervasive anger and frustration or utters statements of hopelessness, or has a litany of endless grievances, either articulated or formally filed in the workplace or in the courts.

All of these, individually and certainly collectively, point to bubbling frustration and a greater likelihood for violence. Leading threat analysis expert Gavin de Becker created the four-point scale JACA, which stands for its four main features, to evaluate the likelihood that a threat will be carried out:

- *Justification:* We first consider whether the person likely feels he is justified to use violence to inflict pain, harm, or death.
- *Alternatives:* We then view whether the person feels he has options other than violence to achieve his means. If violence seems like the only way for him to get justice, he will evaluate the consequences.
- *Consequences:* He assesses the likely repercussions of resorting to violence and weighs whether the probable outcome—injury, death, jail—is worth it.
- *Ability:* Whether his plans for revenge remain a fantasy or turn into a horrid reality hinges on whether he feels he has the means and ability to carry out the threat. If he believes that he does, he will likely move forward.

Linguistic analysis provides another layer of insight. The following passage is a real-life writing sample that is full of *qualifiers* but lacks a single *retractor* (see chapter 5 for elaboration). Findings show that this language pattern suggests that "once an answer to a problem has been found, there may be no turning back."[5] It is also written with *detachment* (see chapter 12), which tells us that he has already distanced himself from his actions. Not long after this note was written, its author murdered his wife.

> I now find myself with a definitive problem which I wish I could find the answer to. And there doesn't seem to be any definitive answer within myself. The problem within me is something that I do not completely understand—whether or not it's myself or the real thing. I keep playing with the idea that maybe that's the trouble. Maybe I should distract my mind and get my mind on interest of something else of another nature, that I may be able to completely get the thought out of my mind. I think, maybe if I go back to my artwork and concentrate on different phases of learning it, that maybe I come into my interests and alleviate the problem for my mind—do everything I can to cooperate with anyone I can that might be able to help me with this problem. And that the thing may find an answer for itself.[6]

In any situation where you feel something is just not right, trust your instincts. You don't need to point to a reason. Your subconscious has picked up on a threat that your conscious mind has dismissed. To protect yourself, you have to learn to trust yourself.

A Threat to Oneself

Although mental illness does not correlate with violence, suicidal thoughts and behaviors are commonly found at increased rates among individuals with either affective or personality disorders. Suicidal people need professional help—period—ideally, before they become so depressed and hopeless that suicide is an option.[7] The fact that someone is in crisis does not necessarily mean he's on the brink of suicide. These warning signs will help you evaluate the risk: We can apply the same JACA scale here as well. If the person expresses the following sentiments, be on high alert:

- *Justification:* "Life isn't worth living. The pain is too much, and besides, everyone—my family, friends, and loved ones—would be better off without me."
- *Alternatives:* "There's nothing I can do to make it better, and I feel like there is no way out."
- *Consequences:* "I won't be around to deal with anything afterward."
- *Ability:* "I have access to (or intend to obtain) weapons or pills. I have made plans and have gotten my affairs in order. I've paid off debts and given away my personal possessions."

A suicidal gesture is a suicide attempt in which the person has no intent to die; for example, the person may take a nonlethal dose of sleeping pills or cut themselves in ways not likely to cause imminent death. The intent of a suicidal gesture is generally to express despair or helplessness or utter a cry for help in an effort to improve one's life, not to die. In some cases, a suicidal gesture may be an attempt to make a dramatic statement or "get even with someone."

That said, intentional self-harm even without suicidal intent is associated with a long-term risk for committing suicide.

Suicidal attempts and gestures can look a lot alike. A suicidal attempt may be a failed suicide (e.g., the person ingested a bottle of pills with the intent to die, but someone intervened, called an ambulance, and the person woke up alive in the hospital, having had their stomach pumped). We can never know when a person will make that fateful decision to take drastic and destructive action, but two indicators

brightly illuminate the already-
lit warning sign.

Major Stressor

In our own lives, whether we
reach for a carton of ice cream
or a bottle of wine, or engage in
otherwise self-destructive behavior, it's generally the result
of a stressor. Most violent behavior follows a stressor, too,
which invariably boils down to
feeling overwhelmed—submerged by our thoughts and emotions. A
stressor may present as any number of issues: a recent financial or personal crisis (such as a bankruptcy), a separation, a restraining order, a
custody battle or hearing, a run-in with the police, a firing or demotion,
and the like. Any significant negative shift in his life or lifestyle, com-
bined with other factors, is legitimate cause for concern.

> When it comes to investments,
> we are reminded that "past
> performance may not be
> indicative of future results," but
> with people, you can expect
> that past performance may well
> indicate future results.

The Copycat Effect

Recent news stories and media coverage about workplace violence can
trigger others to act similarly when they identify with the perpetrator
and share his frustrations. The impact of social influence is even more
concerning and disturbing in an age when technology streams the world
to our fingertips. The media calls it the "copycat effect," but to psycholo-
gists it's the "Werther effect." It is based on the principle that human
beings use others' actions to decide what is proper behavior for themselves.[8]

For example, when people learn of another's suicide, a number of
them decide that suicide may make sense for them, too—oddly, even

some who were not actively planning to end their lives. Some will commit suicide without caring that people know they killed themselves, but others do not want their deaths to appear to be suicides. Thus, research has shown that three days following a report in the media about a suicide, the rate of automobile fatalities increases by 31 percent.[9] This chilling effect extends beyond numbers, in that fatalities are most frequent in the region where the suicide story is publicized, and the more similar we are to the victim, the more likely we are to be influenced (due to ego identification). Hence, when the media reports that a young person has committed suicide, the number of crashes by young people increases. When news about an older person committing suicide is reported, the number of crashes by older individuals increases. Pay particular attention, then, when someone voices empathy or understanding for such actions (e.g., "There's only so much a person can take"; "I'm sure he tried other ways to cope but just ran out of options").

Ernest Hemingway writes, "When people talk, listen completely. Most people never listen." Someone who presents a danger to themselves or to others is screaming in pain. If you listen for it, you will hear it. Loud and clear.

What to Do with What You Know

When all is said and done, we live in a world that has become increasingly chaotic and unpredictable. I hope that, in a worthwhile and meaningful way, the strategies you've learned in this book will give you more confidence, comfort, and security as you move through life. Perhaps, too, in your quest to better learn and predict the behaviors of those around you, you will come to understand more about yourself and possibly what you can do to optimize your own emotional health and the quality of your relationships.

They say that *knowledge is power*. It is not. Knowledge is a tool, like any other. How we wield it makes all of the difference. Real power is the responsible application of knowledge. Knowing what people really think and feel will certainly help you save time, money, energy, and heartache. But it will also position you to better understand, help, and heal those who are in pain.

It is with high hope and expectation that the techniques in this book will be used responsibly, to enlighten, empower, and inspire. They are not designed merely to give you an advantage but also to educate, so that you can become more effective in your life and interactions and more optimistic about your abilities and your possibilities.

Notes

Introduction

1. An astounding 75 percent of law enforcement professionals believe that an averted gaze indicates deception, even though it has been found to be an unreliable indicator. See L. Akehurst, G. Kohnken, A. Vrij, and R. Bull, "Lay Persons' and Police Officers' Beliefs regarding Deceptive Behavior," *Applied Cognitive Psychology* 10, no. 6 (1996): 461–73.

2. Those methods that employ linguistic analysis are ideally used: (a) when the subject is fluent in the language he's speaking or writing in and (b) for longer statements or conversations, rather than a short message, such as a text, because people are often grammatically lax in such exchanges. Moreover, culture, gender, age, education, and socioeconomic status all impact a person's use of language, and a lengthier interaction or longer sample size will allow you to better filter these variances.

Chapter 1

1. Mark Murphy, *Hiring for Attitude: A Revolutionary Approach to Recruiting and Selecting People with Both Tremendous Skills and Superb Attitude,* 1st ed. (New York: McGraw-Hill Education, 2016), 117-18.

2. Ibid., 7.

3. We remind ourselves that we must consider a multitude of factors before making any assumptions. In this instance, for example, the tailor may take great pride in his work, and feelings of extreme shame may temporarily override his otherwise stellar integrity.

4. See Clea Wright Whelan, Graham F. Wagstaff, and Jacqueline M. Wheatcroft, "High-Stakes Lies: Verbal and Nonverbal Cues to Deception in Public Appeals for Help with Missing or Murdered Relatives," *Psychiatry, Psychology and Law* 21, no. 4 (2014): 523–37; doi: 10.1080/13218719 .2013.839931.

5. Morton Wiener and Albert Mehrabian, *Language within Language: Immediacy, a Channel in Verbal Communication* (New York: Appleton-Century-Crofts, 1968).

6. Walter Weintraub, *Verbal Behavior: Adaptation and Psychopathology* (New York: Springer, 1981).

7. Daniel Casasanto and Kyle Jasmin, "Good and Bad in the Hands of Politicians: Spontaneous Gestures during Positive and Negative Speech," *PLoS ONE* 5, no. 7 (2010): e11805; doi: 10.1371/journal.pone.0011805.

Chapter 2

1. An exception is with a condition known as *Stockholm syndrome*, whereby the victim develops a psychological alliance with their abductor.

2. Benjamin H. Seider, Gilad Hirschberger, Kristin L. Nelson, and Robert W. Levenson, "We Can Work It Out: Age Differences in Relational Pronouns, Physiology, and Behavior in Marital Conflict," *Psychology and Aging* 24, no. 3 (2009): 604–13; doi: 10.1037/a0016950.

3. Ibid.

4. James W. Pennebaker, *The Secret Life of Pronouns: What Our Words Say about Us* (New York: Bloomsbury Press, 2011).

5. Christopher Quinn, "Technique Sets the Truth Free" *Orlando Sentinel*, September 23, 1991. Retrieved on June 5, 2019: https://www.orlando sentinel.com/news/os-xpm-1991-09-23-9109230167-story.html.

6. Ibid.

7. We tend to associate vertical placement with power, both literally and metaphorically. Whenever a person is asked to illustrate social or workplace dynamics, they often use vertical positioning and place the more powerful person or group toward the top and the more powerless toward the bottom. This provides ample insight into how people view themselves and others within any interpersonal structure. See T. W. Schubert, "Your Highness: Vertical Positions as Perceptual Symbols of Power," *Journal of Personality and Social Psychology* 89, no. 1 (2005): 1–21; doi: 10.1037/0022 -3514.89.1.1.

Chapter 3

1. James W. Pennebaker, *The Secret Life of Pronouns: What Our Words Say about Us* (New York: Bloomsbury Press, 2011).

2. A. L. Gonzales, J. T. Hancock, and J. W. Pennebaker, "Language Style Matching as a Predictor of Social Dynamics in Small Groups," *Communication Research* 37, no. 1 (2010): 3–19; and P. J. Taylor and S. Thomas, "Linguistic Style Matching and Negotiation Outcome," *Negotiation and Conflict Management Research* 1 (2008): 263–81.

3. Some adverbs are function words (e.g., *then* and *why*).

4. C. K. Chung and J. W. Pennebaker, "The Psychological Functions of Function Words," in *Social Communication: Frontiers of Social Psychology,* ed. K. Fiedler (New York: Psychology Press, 2007), 343–59; and A. S. Meyer and K. Bock, "Representations and Processes in the Production of Pronouns: Some Perspectives from Dutch," *Journal of Memory and Language* 41, no. 2 (1999): 281–301.

5. We learned that words may trigger an intense emotional reaction, and in such instances an individual may use function words to avoid "naming names." A person with a spider phobia who finds one crawling up her leg, is more likely to shout "Get it off!" than "Get this spider off of me!" Parenthetically, some adult children have the unsettling habit of calling a parent by their first name, not always, but often, because they don't want to feel connected and *mom* and *dad* represent a relationship.

6. The line from the cult classic movie *Planet of the Apes* (1968) comes to mind: "Take your stinking paws off me, you damn dirty ape!"

7. A skilled con artist will try to sidle up next to you rather than speak across from you. The reason is that when you are side by side, you have a common perspective, where you quite literally see the world with the same outlook and, as such, create an artificially close relationship.

8. James W. Pennebaker, Matthias R. Mehl, and Kate G. Niederhoffer, "Psychological Aspects of Natural Language Use: Our Words, Our Selves," *Annual Review of Psychology* 54 (2003): 547–77; doi: 10.1146/annurev .psych.54.101601.145041.

Chapter 4

1. Penelope Brown and Stephen C. Levinson, *Politeness: Some Universals in Language Usage* (Cambridge: Cambridge University Press, 1987).

2. Steven Pinker, *The Stuff of Thought: Language as a Window into Human Nature* (New York: Viking, 2007).

3. Research finds that politeness, as a linguistic tool, appears to be universal across all cultures. See Brown and Levinson, *Politeness*.

4. James W. Pennebaker, *The Secret Life of Pronouns: What Our Words Say about Us* (New York: Bloomsbury Press, 2011).

5. Equally surprising, although logically consistent, is that narcissism is unrelated to using first-person singular pronouns. Although narcissists are self-absorbed, they maintain a feeling of superiority, which then orients their focus outwardly. See N. S. Holtzman, A. M. Tackman, A. L. Carey, M. S. Brucks, A. C. P. Küfner, F. G. Deters, M. D. Back, M. B. Donnellan, J. W. Pennebaker, R. A. Sherman, and M. R. Mehl, "Linguistic Markers of Grandiose Narcissism: A LIWC Analysis of 15 Samples," *Journal of Language and Social Psychology* 38, nos. 5–6 (2019): 773–86; doi: 10.1177/ 0261927X19871084.

6. The only way to convey insincerity would be to exaggerate the apology with a mocking tone (e.g., "I am so sorry" read slowly as "I . . . am . . . soooooo sorry . . .").

7. The jutting of the chin presents as an aggressive movement, and even the slight forward thrust of the chin registers as a universal hostile act. See Desmond Morris, *Bodytalk: The Meaning of Human Gestures* (New York: Crown, 1995).

Chapter 5

1. In a life-threatening situation, our mind automatically filters out unnecessary information and stimuli. When driving in a dangerous snowstorm, for example, most people will turn off the radio because it is a needless distraction. Of course, it doesn't help us see out through the windshield, but it does allow our cognitive resources to focus directly on the current threat.

2. Because we often rely on tone of voice to decipher the hidden message, sarcasm doesn't translate well in the written word, even with an apt emoticon.

3. M. Lalljee and M. Cook, "Filled Pauses and Floor-Holding: The Final Test?," *Semiotica* 12 (1975): 219–25.

4. Walter Weintraub, *Verbal Behavior: Adaptation and Psychopathology* (New York: Springer, 1981).

5. Such a state encompasses both physiological response (e.g., raised pulse, increased breathing) and psychological response (e.g., fear and cognitive distortions).

6. Ibid.

7. See David J. Lieberman, *Make Peace with Anyone: Breakthrough Strategies to Quickly End Any Conflict, Feud, or Estrangement* (New York: St. Martin's Press, 2002).

8. See David J. Lieberman, *Never Get Angry Again: The Foolproof Way to Stay Calm and in Control in Any Conversation or Situation* (New York: St. Martin's Press, 2017).

9. Weintraub, *Verbal Behavior.*

10. R. A. Simmons, D. L. Chambless, and P. C. Gordon, "How Do Hostile and Emotionally Overinvolved Relatives View Relationships? What Relatives' Pronoun Use Tells Us," *Family Process* 47, no. 3 (2008): 405–19.

11. Ibid.

12. Walter Weintraub, *Verbal Behavior in Everyday Life* (New York: Springer, 1989).

Chapter 6

1. W. Güth, R. Schmittberger, and B. Schwarze, "An Experimental Analysis of Ultimatum Bargaining," *Journal of Economic Behavior and Organization* 3, no. 4 (1982): 367–88.

2. Joanna Schug, David Matsumoto, Yutaka Horita, Toshio Yamagishi, and Kemberlee Bonnet, "Emotional Expressivity as a Signal of Cooperation," *Evolution and Human Behavior* 31, no. 2 (2010): 87–94; doi: 10.1016/j .evolhumbehav.2009.09.006.

3. The expression "playing it close to the vest" refers to a person who keeps his motivations secret; it comes from a poker saying: "Hold your cards close to your 'vest' [or body]," so other players won't see your cards.

4. Schug, Matsumoto, Horita, Yamagishi, and Bonnet, "Emotional Expressivity as a Signal of Cooperation."

5. Although we cannot presume that the absence of such narration indicates an uncooperative state, the presence of the narration is instructive.

6. Traditional interrogation protocol accomplishes this by taking a small step toward the person. By encroaching ever so slightly into their physical space, you force your subject to move toward a more psychologically defensive posture.

7. Accused of a sexual assault, the suspect emphatically declares, "I have two daughters myself," the assumption being that he would never commit such a heinous crime. His reasoning is as nonsensical as an accused bank robber stating that he has too much respect for money to steal from someone else. Beware "proof of innocence" that isn't proof of anything.

8. If the person is asked the same question time and again—which happens on a witness stand or in a deposition—then self-referral statements should not be construed as an attempt to mislead.

Chapter 7

1. D. R. Carney, A. J. C. Cuddy, and A. J. Yap, "Power Posing: Brief Nonverbal Displays Affect Neuroendocrine Levels and Risk Tolerance," *Psychological Science* 21, no. 10 (2010): 1363–68; doi: 10.1177/0956797610383437.

2. P. Briñol, R. E. Petty, and B. Wagner, "Body Posture Effects on Self-Evaluation: A Self-Validation Approach," *European Journal of Social Psychology* 39, no. 6 (2009): 1053–64.

3. The thinking is not completely faulty because there is a phenomenon called *regression toward the mean.*

4. These insights—about impression management—have now made their way to Homeland Security briefing materials. *The FBI Law Enforcement Bulletin,* vol. 70, no. 7 (Washington, D.C.: U.S. Federal Bureau of Investigation, July 2001). Retrieved on November 17, 2020: https://www.hsdl.org/?abstract&did=447482.

5. A call comes in: "There's a bomb in your building!" Although such a threat should always be taken seriously, the statistical likelihood of there being an actual bomb is slim. In fact, 99.9 percent of all telephone bomb threats are just that—threats. The caller's intent is to cause anxiety and panic.

6. Gavin de Becker, *The Gift of Fear: Survival Signals That Protect Us from Violence* (New York: Little, Brown, 1997).

Chapter 8

1. Intense fear is not bound by time. When a person recalls a traumatic time and the same negative feelings arise, the fight-flight-freeze response activates as if it's happening in real time. At the same time, vivid detail may be absent due to the subconscious coping mechanism, disassociation. See A. Jacobs-Kayam and R. Lev-Wiesel, "In Limbo: Time Perspective and Memory Deficit among Female Survivors of Sexual Abuse," *Frontiers in Psychology* (April 2019); doi: 10.3389/fpsyg.2019.00912.

2. In certain circumstances, all requests and commands should be positively phrased for optimum compliance. For example, to a small child pouring milk, it is better to say, "Hold the glass straight" or "Pour slowly," rather

than, "Don't tip the glass" or "Not so fast." Those in law enforcement are likewise trained to issue commands such as "Freeze" instead of "Don't move," and "Stay down" rather than "Don't get up."

3. David J. Lieberman, *Never Be Lied to Again: How to Get the Truth in Five Minutes or Less in Any Conversation or Situation*. Unabridged. Macmillan Audio, 2018 (New York: St. Martin's Press, 1998).

Chapter 9

1. G. Kuhn, H. A. Caffaratti, R. Teszka, and R. A. Rensink, "A Psychologically-Based Taxonomy of Misdirection," *Frontiers in Psychology* 5 (2014): 1392; doi: 10.3389/fpsyg.2014.01392.

2. Amos Tversky and Daniel Kahneman, "Availability: A Heuristic for Judging Frequency and Probability," *Cognitive Psychology* 5, no. 2 (1973): 207–32; doi:10.1016/0010-0285(73)90033-9.

3. Robert B. Cialdini, *Influence: The Psychology of Persuasion* (New York: HarperBusiness, 2006), 225.

4. John A. Bargh, Mark Chen, and Lara Burrows, "Automaticity of Social Behavior: Direct Effects of Trait Construct and Stereotype Activation on Action," *Journal of Personality and Social Psychology* 71, no. 2 (1996): 230–44.

5. David J. Lieberman, *Never Be Lied to Again: How to Get the Truth in Five Minutes or Less in Any Conversation or Situation* (New York: St. Martin's Press, 1998).

6. Wu Youyou, David Stillwell, H. Andrew Schwartz, and Michal Kosinski, "Birds of a Feather Do Flock Together: Behavior-Based Personality-Assessment Method Reveals Personality Similarity among Couples and Friends," *Psychological Science* 28, no. 3 (2017): 276–84; doi: 10.1177/0956797616678187.

7. D. Drachman, A. DeCarufel, and C. A. Insko, "The Extra Credit Effect in Interpersonal Attraction," *Journal of Experimental Social Psychology* 14, no. 5 (1978): 458–65.

8. Maria Konnikova, *The Confidence Game: Why We Fall for It . . . Every Time* (New York: Viking, 2016).

9. Ibid.

10. Robert B. Cialdini, *Pre-suasion: A Revolutionary Way to Influence and Persuade* (New York: Simon & Schuster, 2018), 7.

Chapter 10

1. Walter Weintraub, *Verbal Behavior: Adaptation and Psychopathology* (New York: Springer, 1981).

2. A personality disorder is a way of thinking, feeling, and behaving that deviates from cultural expectations, causes distress or problems in functioning, and lasts over time. See *Diagnostic and Statistical Manual of Mental Disorders*, 5th ed. (DSM-5) (VA: American Psychiatric Association, 2013).

3. When the ego is fed with power, control, money, or some similar fuel, it generally puts us into a good mood, and so our attitude and behavior temporarily shift to mimic someone with higher self-esteem.

4. The natures of men and women, compounded by cultural influences, are demonstrated by linguistic differences—whereby women tend to use language that is, on average, more passive and polite. Should one's emotional health become severely compromised, the trajectory is consistent with findings that show that women are approximately twice as likely than men to experience depression.

5. Alternatively, this language may also indicate a guard who is speaking to someone of higher status. Even though the guard maintains the authority to refuse entry to a specific area, they conduct themselves properly within the status hierarchy and thus use deferential language.

6. A. A. Augustine, M. R. Mehl, and R. J. Larsen, "A Positivity Bias in Written and Spoken English, and Its Moderation by Personality and Gender," *Social Psychology and Personality Science* 2, no. 5 (2011): 508–15; and T. Yarkoni, "Personality in 100,000 Words: A Large-Scale Analysis of Personality and Word Use among Bloggers," *Journal of Research in Personality* 44, no. 3 (2010): 363–73; doi: 10.1016/j.jrp.2010.04.001.

7. Yarkoni, "Personality in 100,000 Words."

8. H. A. Schwartz, J. C. Eichstaedt, L. Dziurzynski, M. L. Kern, E. Blanco, M. Kosinski, D. Stillwell, M. E. P. Seligman, and L. H. Ungar, "Toward Personality Insights from Language Exploration in Social Media," 2013 AAAI Spring Symposium Series: Analyzing Microtext, Stanford, CA.

9. Ibid.

10. Ibid.

11. In chapter 14, we will learn that in gauging emotional health, we're often looking for the middle of the road, which means balance and moderation. Saying *thank you* when proper and necessary is an indication of mental fitness. But extreme overuse is as questionable as its total absence.

12. C. S. Lewis, *Reflections on the Psalms* (New York: Harcourt, Brace, 1958), 93–97.

13. Findings show that gratitude can also reduce the frequency, duration, and intensity of depressive episodes. This is because giving and gratitude (which is itself giving—giving thanks) redirect our attention away from ourselves. When we look for ways to say thanks instead of indulging what may be our more natural impulse to complain, we break down the neural net of anger, frustration, and resentment. See A. M. Wood, S. Joseph, and J. Maltby, "Gratitude Uniquely Predicts Satisfaction with Life: Incremental Validity above the Domains and Facets of the Five Factor Model," *Personality and Individual Differences* 45, no. 1 (2008): 49–54.

Chapter 11

1. Are they judging you? Do they think you're a fool? Maybe. But understand, we all see the world through the lens with which we need to see it. You do it. They do it. We all do it. Their own stuff forces the narrative about you. If their self-esteem is healthy, then their thoughts are compassionate and nonjudgmental. The ego judges to secure its narrative. Otherwise, the person would just have empathy for you—and love and accept

you and recognize that your behavior is largely a product of your stuff. In other words, they would feel your pain and not seek to apply more.

2. Daniel Kahneman, *Thinking, Fast and Slow* (New York: Farrar, Straus & Giroux, 2011).

3. Few interactions are immune. Research finds that a clinician's own personality can hamper their ability to accurately assess psychological disorders. To put it another way, their analysis echoes aspects of their personality. Physicians who themselves were classified as anxious were more likely to document an anxiety or depression diagnosis than their peers. See Paul R. Duberstein, B. Chapman, R. Epstein, K. McCollumn, and R. Kravitz, "Physician Personality Characteristics and Inquiry about Mood Symptoms in Primary Care," *Journal of General Internal Medicine* 23, no. 11 (2008): 1791–95.

4. D. Wood, P. Harms, and S. Vazire, "Perceiver Effects as Projective Tests: What Your Perceptions of Others Say about You," *Journal of Personality and Social Psychology* 99, no. 1 (2010): 174–90.

5. Ibid.

6. "Smoke Alarms Using Mother's Voice Wake Children Better than High-Pitch Tone Alarms" (press release), Nationwide Children's. Retrieved on August 30, 2019: https://www.nationwidechildrens.org/newsroom/news-releases/2018/10/smoke-alarm-study.

7. The RAS regulates awareness and arousal and orients to what we deem significant. This means that our antenna is up for both what we fear and what we desire. For instance, a jungle guide is tuned in to the people on his tour (a desire to ensure their welfare) as well as to potential threats (out of fear).

8. Jonathan M. Adler, Erica D. Chin, Aiswarya P. Kolisetty, and Thomas F. Oltmanns, "The Distinguishing Characteristics of Narrative Identity in Adults with Features of Borderline Personality Disorder: An Empirical Investigation," *Journal of Personality Disorders* 26, no. 4 (2012): 498–512.

9. D. P. McAdams, A. Diamond, E. de St. Aubin, and E. Mansfield, "Stories of Commitment: The Psychosocial Construction of Generative Lives,"

Journal of Personality and Social Psychology 72, no. 3 (1997): 678–94; doi: 1997-07966-018.

Chapter 12

1. The notable exception is the submissive who perpetually apologizes, even when she is not at fault. Due to extreme low self-esteem, she doesn't feel worthy enough to stand up for herself and gives in to assuage feelings of misplaced guilt and shame or out of fear of disconnection or emotional retribution.

2. Thomas Szasz, *The Untamed Tongue: A Dissenting Dictionary* (La Salle, IL: Open Court, 1990).

3. We may engage in this thinking on a wholesale level, often blaming our parents for the issues we have today, while maintaining that they operated with willful intent. We don't factor their upbringing into the equation when considering their behavior toward us. It continues with our own children, whereby we are the only ones who are products of our environment, our choices handcuffed by our upbringing, while all the people around us choose to behave the way they do.

4. We would not assume a character flaw within ourselves—"I don't care about others" or "I'm just a jerk"—unless our self-concept includes such behavior, in which case our actions become a badge of honor and "This is who I am."

5. The more accepting we are of ourselves, the more accepting we are of others. Areas where we don't accept ourselves are revealed in our intolerance for others, which often plays out in parenting. It is not uncommon for a parent to be most frustrated by the child who is most similiar to them. The child holds a mirror to what the parent is unable to accept in themselves.

6. J. Jaffe, "Communication Networks in Freud's Interview Technique," *Psychiatric Quarterly* 32, no. 3 (1958): 456–73; doi: 10.1007/BF01563516.

7. Ibid.

Chapter 13

1. We often experience more pain when we feel disrespected by a smart, wealthy, or attractive person. Via the ego, we believe that this individual has more value, and so his treatment of us is of greater significance.

2. C. S. Lewis, *Reflections on the Psalms* (New York: Harcourt, Brace, 1958), 93–97.

3. Viktor E. Frankl, *The Unheard Cry for Meaning: Psychotherapy and Humanism* (New York: Simon & Schuster, 1978); and Sigmund Freud, *Civilization and Its Discontents*, trans. and ed. J. Strachey (New York: W. W. Norton, 1961).

4. Peter Schmuck, Tim Kasser, and Richard M. Ryan, "Intrinsic and Extrinsic Goals: Their Structure and Relationship to Well-Being in German and U.S. College Students," *Social Indicators Research* 50, no. 2 (2000): 225–41.

5. Abraham H. Maslow, *Motivation and Personality* (New York: Harper & Row, 1954), 46. Unbeknownst to many, in his later years Maslow amended his five-tier model to include a sixth tier, which places self-transcendence as a level higher than self-actualization. He writes, "The self only finds its actualization in giving itself to some higher goal outside oneself, in altruism and spirituality." A. H. Maslow, "The Further Reaches of Human Nature," *Journal of Transpersonal Psychology* 1, no. 1 (1969): 1–9.

Chapter 14

1. P. Resnik, W. Armstrong, L. Claudino, and T. Nguyen, "The University of Maryland CLPsych 2015 Shared Task System," *Proceedings of the Second Workshop on Computational Linguistics and Clinical Psychology: From Linguistic Signal to Clinical Reality* (2015): 54–60; doi: 10.3115/v1/W15-1207.

2. Ernest Dichter, *Handbook of Consumer Motivations: The Psychology of the World of Objects* (New York: McGraw-Hill, 1964).

3. When we face a choice between smaller rewards and larger but delayed rewards, emotional distress causes us to shift toward the former. See W. Mischel, E. B. Ebbesen, and A. Raskoff Zeiss, "Cognitive and Atten-

tional Mechanisms in Delay of Gratification," *Journal of Personality and Social Psychology* 21, no. 2 (1972): 204–18.

4. Isaiah 22:12.

5. The distinction is that on a date, negotiation, interview, and so forth, anxiety is inversely correlated to one's confidence and interest level. This means the less confident a person is and the more they want "it," the more anxious they will become. When it comes to life stressors, the person who is less confident (and thus lacks agency—the belief that he can be effective) and who presumably wants to succeed will become more anxious. Evidence of this is that a person who is severely depressed will exhibit very little or no anxiety in typically stressful situations because they simply do not care. Although they have low confidence, they also have zero interest in life itself.

6. G. Alan Marlatt and Judith R. Gordon, eds., *Relapse Prevention: Maintenance Strategies in the Treatment of Addictive Behaviors* (New York: Guilford Press, 1985); and R. Sinha, "Modeling Stress and Drug Craving in the Laboratory: Implications for Addiction Treatment Development," *Addiction Biology* 14, no. 1 (2009): 84–98.

7. R. Sinha, "The Role of Stress on Addiction Relapse," *Current Psychiatry Reports* 9, no. 5 (2007): 388–95; and K. Witkiewitz and N. A. Villarroel, "Dynamic Association between Negative Affect and Alcohol Lapses Following Alcohol," *Journal of Consulting and Clinical Psychology* 77, no. 4 (2009): 633–44.

8. D. C. Vinson and V. Arelli, "State Anger and the Risk of Injury: A Case-Control and Case-Crossover Study," *Annals of Family Medicine* 4, no. 1 (2006): 63–68.

9. William Glasser, *Reality Therapy: A New Approach to Psychiatry* (New York: Harper Perennial, 1975).

10. K. R. Merikangas, N. J. Risch, and M. M. Weissman, "Comorbidity and Co-transmission of Alcoholism, Anxiety and Depression," *Psychological Medicine* 24, no. 1 (1994): 69–80; doi: 10.1017/S0033291700026842.

Chapter 15

1. J. M. Adler, A. F. Turner, K. M. Brookshier, C. Monahan, I. Walder-Biesanz, L. H. Harmeling, M. Albaugh, D. P. McAdams, and T. F. Oltmanns, "Variation in Narrative Identity Is Associated with Trajectories of Mental Health over Several Years," *Journal of Personality and Social Psychology* 108, no. 3 (2015): 476–96; doi: 10.1037/a0038601.

2. D. P. McAdams, J. Reynolds, M. Lewis, A. H. Patten, and P. J. Bowman, "When Bad Things Turn Good and Good Things Turn Bad: Sequences of Redemption and Contamination in Life Narrative and Their Relation to Psychosocial Adaptation in Midlife Adults and in Students," *Personality and Social Psychology Bulletin* 27, no. 4 (2001): 474–85.

3. The poorer one's emotional health, the greater the likelihood that an experience will be tainted by a tangential event. The drizzle of rain that "ruined" the whole picnic is causal, but getting a speeding ticket driving home from an otherwise sunny-day picnic retroactively casts the picnic as "bad."

4. The obstacle that is reframed as a stepping-stone is not a matter of looking through rose-colored glasses but of seeing something in a new way. The experience is a function of perspective, and with a new perspective comes a new context and thus a new meaning.

5. S. S. Tomkins, "Script Theory," in *The Emergence of Personality,* ed. J. Aronoff, A. I. Rabin, and R. A. Zucker (New York: Springer, 1987), 147–216.

6. Monika Obrębska and Joanna Zinczuk-Zielazna, "Explainers as an Indicator of Defensive Attitude to Experienced Anxiety in Young Women Differing in Their Styles of Coping with Threatening Stimuli," *Psychology of Language and Communication* 21, no. 1 (2017): 34–50; doi: 10.1515/plc-2017-0003.

7. All-or-nothing thinking is called *splitting,* which is a defense mechanism characterized by a polarization of attitudes, values, and beliefs. Unable to tolerate opposing shades of gray (e.g., decent and moral people can, at times, act wrongly; not all opportunities are either a "can't miss" or a "total scam"; everything isn't ruined because something isn't perfect), the world is not only neatly cataloged but also labeled in extremes.

8. Absolutist language is also found in people who are recovering from depression (which means they are still vulnerable or susceptible), but the content of speech is more positive. See M. Al-Mosaiwi and T. Johnstone, "In an Absolute State: Elevated Use of Absolutist Words Is a Marker Specific to Anxiety, Depression, and Suicidal Ideation," *Clinical Psychological Science* 6, no. 4 (2018): 529–42; doi: 10.1177/2167702617747074.

9. The attributes and language of emotionally unstable people can usually be characterized as behaviors that exemplify emotional immaturity. In other words, they behave as you'd expect children to behave—throwing sudden tantrums, erupting in mindless exuberance, having wild mood swings, and insisting on an absolute, black-or-white view of events. Therefore, techniques used to gauge a person's emotional stability are applicable only to adults. Children are egocentric by nature; it is normal for them to see their world through the lens of "I." A child's natural egocentricity and narrowed perspective are part of a normal and even healthy emotional landscape. On this account, children do not typically receive a diagnosis for a personality disorder.

10. H. Peters, "Degree Adverbs in Early Modern English," *Studies in Early Modern English*, 13 (1994): 269–88.

11. Al-Mosaiwi and Johnstone, "In an Absolute State."

12. The state can be induced by something completely unrelated, and the person's mood carries over into his current behavior, or the state may be a function of an emotional flash point, in which case his animated intensity comes from his passion within the situation; but again, neither speaks specifically to trait personality.

13. We all have our blind spots, areas of life where we do not see what is obvious to others. It seems so ridiculous to us when others act irrationally, only because their blind spots are different than ours. We are just as irrational—more so, in fact, if we choose not to accept this fact and instead become angry when another does not see our point of view. Emotional health allows for empathy because the ego does not need to fortify itself with anger and animosity. We might believe that a person is misguided, ignorant, and certainly wrong, but it is the ego and underlying insecurities that stoke the ember of fear into full-blown anger. In other words, we can recognize an injustice and become impassioned for a cause, in which case we move forward rationally and productively; but when the ego mobilizes, anger and animosity hijack the thought process. No one ever walked away from a conversation and thought, *I wish I would have gotten angrier; I would have been able to handle myself so much better.*

14. When we believe strongly in something, even the healthiest among us will, at times, become impassioned and emphatic. We feel that others should see things the way that we do. There is, of course, nothing wrong with that. We cross the line of emotional health when everything is put into the basket of "my way or the highway." Such a person cannot question herself, which means that no one else can, either. It's not just politics and religion, but which flavor of ice cream is "the best." Such a person is overly sensitive, easily insulted, and takes offense to just about anything and anyone who dares to see things differently than she does. For this reason, a benign interaction is more telling of a person's emotional health because nothing other than an overinflated ego is in danger. The more significant the situation, the more likely real-world ramifications are to come into play and thus offer logical justification to hold one's ground and defend one's thinking.

Chapter 16

1. Seth Rosenthal, "The Fine Line between Confidence and Arrogance: Investigating the Relationship of Self-Esteem to Narcissism," *Dissertation Abstracts International* 66, no. 5-B (2005): 2868.

2. D. S. Ryan, "Self-Esteem: An Operational Definition and Ethical Analysis," *Journal of Psychology and Theology* 11, no. 4 (1983): 295–302.

3. Let's unpack the psychology with a parable. Imagine that a king allows you to live in his palace. He provides his finest servants to tend to your every whim, his finest tailors to make closets full of clothing, and his finest chefs to prepare your favorite dishes. Could you even conceive of asking for more? Would you not be too embarrassed to demand a finer fabric or a fluffier pillow? This is humility. Humility comes from the recognition that whatever you may have, everything you have is abundant beyond imagination. When you live with this awareness, you become filled with gratitude and bursting with abundance and cannot conceive of taking, but only of giving.

4. The arrogant mentality looks at the net gain to their self-worth, meaning "what I have added to myself that makes me more valuable." For example, a salesperson may meet with a hundred rejections during the day, but he focuses on the single yes that makes a sale. The other type of person is injured by the rejection. He feels less worthy, and so, after receiving a few nos, the pain is too much for him. This is not to say the first person is emotionally healthier, only that the rejections are not as scary as the fear of not earning money, which he feels makes him more valuable.

5. J. M. Adams, D. Florell, K. Alex Burton, and W. Hart, "Why Do Narcissists Disregard Social-Etiquette Norms? A Test of Two Explanations for Why Narcissism Relates to Offensive-Language Use," *Personality and Individual Differences*, 58 (2014): 26–30.

6. Ibid.

7. Ibid.

8. N. S. Holtzman, A. M. Tackman, A. L. Carey, M. S. Brucks, A. C. P. Küfner, F. G. Deters, M. D. Back, James W. Pennebaker, Ryne A. Sherman, and M. R. Mehl, "Linguistic Markers of Grandiose Narcissism: A LIWC Analysis of 15 Samples," *Journal of Language and Social Psychology* 38, nos. 5–6 (2019): 773–86; doi: 10.1177/0261927X19871084.

9. Ibid.

10. W. K. Campbell, E. Rudich, and C. Sedikides, "Narcissism, Self-Esteem, and the Positivity of Self-Views: Two Portraits of Self-Love," *Personality and Social Psychology Bulletin* 28, no. 3 (2002): 358–68.

11. J. T. Cheng, J. L. Tracy, and G. E. Miller, "Are Narcissists Hardy or Vulnerable? The Role of Narcissism in the Production of Stress-Related Biomarkers in Response to Emotional Distress," *Emotion* 13, no. 6 (2013): 1004–11; doi: 10.1037/a0034410.

12. Monika Obrębska and Joanna Zinczuk-Zielazna, "Explainers as an Indicator of Defensive Attitude to Experienced Anxiety in Young Women Differing in Their Styles of Coping with Threatening Stimuli," *Psychology of Language and Communication* 21, no. 1 (2017): 34–50; doi: 10.1515/plc -2017-0003.

13. A person who theoretically has 100 percent self-esteem would have no desire, no need, to control anyone or anything. He recognizes that the only thing he is really in control of is his choice—his ability to exercise self-control. Although our ultimate goal is connection, the fear generated by the ego corrupts the process and mandates control because it tells us the real "I" is not loved and lovable and worthy of connection.

14. Although any given insecurity may make someone more timid or withdrawn, it could equally produce the need to compensate through over-achievement. See Tom Butler-Bowdon, *50 Psychology Classics* (New York: Nicholas Brealey, 2007).

15. Filled with shame, our inner voice says, *I am less.* This is a reflection of the painful belief that we are unworthy of love and undeserving of acceptance—and, by extension, all that we love is neither safe nor secure. Subconsciously, we think, *The real me is unworthy of connection. I will put on a show and become someone who is more lovable so that I will be loved.*

16. The psychological dynamics in play help us understand the plague of childhood stardom. When the celebrity is faced with sudden fame, the gap between his authentic self and his public persona is wide. *Would they still love me if they really knew me?* Likewise, we can better understand why overnight sensations too often unravel emotionally—because the greater the ego or image and the less authentic the individual, the more exposure and vulnerability they feel, which breeds anxiety and oftentimes depression.

17. We know that if a child does not feel he is getting adequate positive attention, he will do what it takes to get negative attention. His requirement for connection, to feel heard and significant, is greater than his desire to be seen as "a good boy." Although being "bad" or "difficult" does not optimize connection, as I explained, this egocentric psyche cannot help but manifest negative traits born out of arrogance, which will no doubt lead to rejection and disconnection. The default of many children, this emotionally immature route seeks out connection by any means necessary.

18. The ego may resort to any and every conceivable and inconceivable length to maintain autonomy, which brings the illusion of control. (In the extreme, it may lead us to kill another person or ourselves.) Whether someone has a personality disorder (ranging from narcissistic personality disorder to paranoid schizophrenic disorder) or an emotional disorder (such as obsessive-compulsive disorder or anorexia nervosa), it is all about control.

Chapter 17

1. Most sociopaths are highly intelligent and high functioning, while psychopaths are typically less intelligent and less equipped to adapt to life's challenges. Sociopaths are likewise more able to control their immediate rage, which makes them more difficult to spot and, subsequently, dangerous.

2. Statistically, men are six times more likely than women to suffer with this disorder, and the majority of people will have developed symptoms by the age of twelve.

3. Hervey M. Cleckley, *The Mask of Sanity: An Attempt to Reinterpret the So-Called Psychopathic Personality* (St. Louis: C. V. Mosby 1941).

4. Although they transcend typical emotions, it is a myth that the sociopath has no fear. They experience what are called proto-emotions, which are basic instincts that permit short bursts of anger or rage when they feel overpowered and helpless.

5. When a person sees an image that shocks or scares them, the fight-flight-freeze response engages and their pupils dilate. This is not the case with a sociopath because their physiological response to threat is diminished, if not altogether absent. Their pupils do not enlarge, which makes this a clear physical marker for this condition. See D. T. Burley, N. S. Gray, and R. J. Snowden, "Emotional Modulation of the Pupil Response in Psychopathy," *Personality Disorders: Theory, Research, and Treatment* 10, no. 4 (2019): 365–75; doi: 10.1037/per0000313.

6. Trust your instincts! Research found that 77.3 percent of people who had interviewed an adult psychopath reported a physiological reaction (sensation of skin crawling, difficulty breathing, frozen muscles). See J. R. Meloy, "Pathologies of Attachment, Violence, and Criminality," in *Handbook of Psychology*, ed. Alan M. Goldstein, vol. 11, *Forensic Psychology* (New York: Wiley, 2002), 509–26.

7. These behaviors are observed in those who have not yet seized control of the person or situation. Sociopaths who are already in a position of power

are extremely dangerous in a workplace environment. They are a wrecking ball to a positive, cooperative culture—they thrive on division, detection, and employ manipulation and outright deceit. And those at the top, with no one to answer to, are utterly ruthless.

8. Gaslighting is a common tactic employed by those who suffer from a personality disorder, and it can happen in both our personal and professional relationships. Through manipulation, distraction, and stealth aggression, victims are left to question their perception of reality—to doubt both themselves and their thinking—and are often left feeling confused, inadequate, and depressed. With their sense of reality and identity undermined, they can feel like they're going crazy.

9. A. Crossley and D. Langdridge, "Perceived Sources of Happiness: A Network Analysis," *Journal of Happiness Studies* 6, no. 2 (2005): 107–35.

Chapter 18

1. William Glasser, *Reality Therapy: A New Approach to Psychiatry* (New York: Harper Perennial, 1975).

2. As lower self-esteem engages the ego, the resultant arrogance creates both a character and a temperament that do not lend themselves to healthy interactions. Rather than foster traits that allow for maximum connection (e.g., humility, kindness, vulnerability, authenticity), egocentricity brings all the delightful personality traits that turn people off and lead to disconnection (e.g., judging, condemning, being critical or argumentative).

3. Empathy is the capacity to share another's emotions and feel their pain rather than merely feel sorry for them. The person with empathy feels grateful for knowing about others' troubles because they genuinely want to alleviate other people's suffering.

4. See R. Krueger, B. Hicks, and M. McGue, "Altruism and Antisocial Behavior: Independent Tendencies, Unique Personality Correlates, Distinct Etiologies," *Psychological Science* 12, no. 5 (2001): 397–403.

5. A person who seeks attention for attention's sake is clearly egocentric, but those who prefer to blend in are not necessarily ego-free. They may be afraid of any attention altogether, which indicates an avoidant personality—

whereby the ego manifestation of either personality or pathology forces them into hiding rather than the spotlight.

6. It is important to yet again qualify that our overall assessment must not rely on single signs or situations. There are some good, decent people who are just absentminded and may forget to return what they borrow. People may understandably lie to protect privacy, avoid being embarrassed, or elude danger to themselves or others. White lies, such as telling a spouse her new hairstyle is great, even though you hate it, are appropriate, healthy, and, most would argue, smart. Moreover, a lie of omission, not revealing a truth that may cause strife between others, is also responsible. But candor or bluntness at someone else's expense, demonstrating little or no sensitivity to any pain he is causing, indicates a person who lacks empathy and perspective.

Chapter 19

1. D. Davis and T. C. Brock, "Use of First Person Pronouns as a Function of Increased Objective Self-Awareness and Performance Feedback," *Journal of Experimental Social Psychology* 11, no. 4 (1975): 389–400.

2. L. A. Lee, D. A. Sbarra, A. E. Mason, and R. W. Law, "Attachment Anxiety, Verbal Immediacy, and Blood Pressure: Results from a Laboratory Analog Study Following Marital Separation," *Personal Relationships* 18, no. 2 (2011): 285–301.

3. A. Aldao, S. Nolen-Hoeksema, and S. Schweizer, "Emotion-Regulation Strategies across Psychopathology: A Meta-Analytic Review," *Clinical Psychology Review* 30, no. 2 (2010): 217–37; doi: 10.1016/j.cpr.2009.11.004; N. Mor and J. Winquist, "Self-Focused Attention and Negative Affect: A Meta-Analysis," *Psychological Bulletin* 128, no. 4 (2002): 638–62; doi: 10.1037/0033-2909.128.4.638; and E. Watkins and R. G. Brown, "Rumination and Executive Function in Depression: An Experimental Study," *Journal of Neurology, Neurosurgery and Psychiatry* 72, no. 3 (2002): 400–2; doi: 10.1136/jnnp.72.3.400.

4. Serotonin is a neurotransmitter found in the brain. It is involved in motor functioning, appetite and sleep control, and hormone regulation. Studies have shown that stress causes an excessive uptake of serotonin. In condi-

tions of continued exposure to stress, this high turnover rate causes depletion of serotonin that may ultimately result in depression. See H. Anisman and R. Zacharko, "Depression: The Predisposing Influence of Stress," *Behavioral and Brain Sciences* 5, no. 1 (1982): 89–137.

5. Daniel Kahneman, *Thinking, Fast and Slow* (New York: Farrar, Straus & Giroux, 2011).

6. The "we" who thinks about it is the ego, which filters our thoughts through a lens of fears and insecurities.

7. W. Bucci and N. Freedman, "The Language of Depression," *Bulletin of the Menninger Clinic* 45, no. 4 (1981): 334–58; and Walter Weintraub, *Verbal Behavior: Adaptation and Psychopathology* (New York: Springer, 1981).

8. David Townsend and Eli Saltz, "Phrases vs Meaning in the Immediate Recall of Sentences," *Psychonomic Science* 29, no. 6 (2013): 381–84; doi: 10.3758/BF03336607.

9. Ibid.

10. M. R. Mehl, M. L. Robbins, and S. E. Holleran, "How Taking a Word for a Word Can Be Problematic: Context-Dependent Linguistic Markers of Extraversion and Neuroticism," paper presented at the 11th Conference of the International Association for Language and Social Psychology, 2008. Tucson, Arizona.

11. P. Resnik, W. Armstrong, L. Claudino, and T. Nguyen, "The University of Maryland CLPsych 2015 Shared Task System," *Proceedings of the Second Workshop on Computational Linguistics and Clinical Psychology: From Linguistic Signal to Clinical Reality* (2015): 54–60; doi: 10.3115/v1/W15 -1207.

12. A. Pusztai and A. Bugán, "Analysis of Suicide Notes from Persons Committing Completed Suicides," *Psychiatria Hungarica* 20, no. 4 (2005): 271–80; and B. Gawda, "The Analysis of Farewell Letters of Suicidal Persons," *Bulletin de la Société des sciences médicales du Grand-Duché de Luxembourg* 1 (2008): 67–74.

13. M. Al-Mosaiwi and T. Johnstone, "In an Absolute State: Elevated Use of Absolutist Words Is a Marker Specific to Anxiety, Depression, and Sui-

cidal Ideation," *Clinical Psychological Science* 6, no. 4 (2018): 529–42; doi: 10.1177/2167702617747074.

14. J. D. Teasdale, J. Scott, R. G. Moore, H. Hayhurst, M. Pope, and E. S. Paykel, "How Does Cognitive Therapy Prevent Relapse in Residual Depression? Evidence from a Controlled Trial," *Journal of Consulting and Clinical Psychology* 69, no. 3 (2001): 347–57.

15. See W. Keith Campbell, Eric A. Rudich, and Constantine Sedikides, "Narcissism, Self-Esteem, and the Positivity of Self-Views: Two Portraits of Self Love," *Personality and Social Psychology Bulletin* 28, no. 3 (2002): 358–68. Retrieved on August 30, 2016: http://psp.sagepub.com/content/28/3/358.short.

16. B. Silvestrini, "Trazodone: From the Mental Pain to the 'Dys-stress' Hypothesis of Depression," *Clinical Neuropharmacology* 12, Suppl. 1, (1989): S4–10. PMID 2568177.

17. Noted physician and pain-management pioneer, Dr. John Sarno explains that many physical ailments are subconsciously induced to move our attention away from less manageable and less containable emotional distress. Their purpose is to deliberately distract the subconscious mind, and they are generated "to assist the process of repression." He explains that physical pain is not the surfacing of hidden emotions but rather manifests to prevent these emotions from becoming conscious. See John E. Sarno, *Healing Back Pain: The Mind-Body Connection* (New York: Grand Central, 1991). John E. Sarno, *The Divided Mind: The Epidemic of Mindbody Disorders* (New York: ReganBooks, 2006), 54.

18. M. Laughlin and R. Johnson, "Premenstrual Syndrome," *101 American Family Physician* 29, no. 3 (2016): 265–69.

19. Weintraub, *Verbal Behavior.*

20. Recall in chapter 5 that *suppression* and *immobilization* are two ways that a person may choose to deal with their anger and become *sad* rather than *mad.* Either of these modes may trigger a depressive episode because feeling sad is a powerful, albeit unhealthy, way to channel anxiety and to restrain one's anger. When one "simply doesn't care," then one can be neither anxious nor angry.

21. Weintraub, *Verbal Behavior.*

22. William Glasser International Newsletter, June 2013, 11. Retrieved on May 11, 2019. Glasser boldly encourages people to be careful with their language and to instead rephrase their emotional state to reflect what is actually happening—we are actively choosing to depress ourselves.

23. Richard Bandler and John Grinder, *The Structure of Magic* (Palo Alto, CA: Science & Behavior Books, 1975).

24. J. M. Adler, "Living into the Story: Agency and Coherence in a Longitudinal Study of Narrative Identity Development and Mental Health over the Course of Psychotherapy," *Journal of Personality and Social Psychology* 102, no. 2 (2012): 367–89; doi: 10.1037/a0025289.

25. J. M. Adler and M. Poulin, "The Political Is Personal: Narrating 9/11 and Psychological Well-Being," *Journal of Personality* 77, no. 4 (2009): 903–32; doi: 10.1111/j.1467- 6494.2009.00569.x.

26. The healthiest mentality is when we put forth our full effort, while recognizing that we do not cause—nor are we in full control of—the outcome. This is quite different from someone who does not feel that his actions will impact, in any way, his happiness and well-being.

27. D. Hiroto, "Locus of Control and Learned Helplessness," *Journal of Experimental Psychology* 102, no. 2 (1974): 187–93.

28. It is not surprising that people demonstrate a greater willingness to take action when feeling empowered compared to feeling helpless. See A. D. Galinsky, D. H. Gruenfeld, and J. C. Magee, "From Power to Action," *Journal of Personality and Social Psychology* 85, no. 3 (2003): 453–66; doi: 10.1037/0022-3514.85.3.453

29. In the extreme, she feels that she is not able to accomplish anything great in her own life, so to seek a purpose she resigns herself to serving the good of others. While this behavior may be the same, the motivation is quite different from those who devote their lives to serving humanity. These people help others because they are passionate and feel that it's their purpose in life. This person does for others at the expense of herself.

30. See Jonathan M. Adler, Erica D. Chin, Aiswarya P. Kolisetty, and Thomas F. Oltmanns, "The Distinguishing Characteristics of Narrative Identity in Adults with Features of Borderline Personality Disorder: An Empirical Investigation," *Journal of Personality Disorders* 26, no. 4 (2012): 498–512.

31. This is not to suggest that these or other mental disorders are not the product of genetics or inborn wiring that would have manifested regardless of trauma or circumstance.

32. Paranoia is an unwanted and unjustified feeling that other people are trying to harm you. Notice: Is the person in question overly suspicious? Does she often misconstrue kind behavior as unfriendly or hostile? Mild paranoia might manifest in the form of someone believing that people are insulting them or "talking about them" behind their back or "trying to deceive" them. Practically, there's not tremendous reason for alarm unless it gets more extreme; delusional thinking (a step beyond paranoia) sounds more like "They're trying to kill me" or "People are trying to kidnap me."

33. At a recent presentation at the National Institute of Mental Health in Bethesda, Maryland, Dr. Guillermo A. Cecchi, of IBM's Thomas J. Watson Research Center, discussed how they and other researchers are engaged in computational linguistics to quantify psychiatric conditions using recordings of speech samples.

34. G. Bedi, F. Carrillo, G. A. Cecchi, D. F. Slezak, M. Sigman, N. B. Mota, S. Ribeiro, D. C. Javitt, M. Copelli, and C. M. Corcoran, "Automated Analysis of Free Speech Predicts Psychosis Onset in High-Risk Youths," *NPJ Schizophrenia* 1, no. 1 (2015): 15030; doi: 10.1038/npjschz.2015.30; and C. E. Bearden, K. N. Wu, R. Caplan, and T. D. Cannon, "Thought Disorder and Communication Deviance as Predictors of Outcome in Youth at Clinical High Risk for Psychosis," *Journal of the American Academy of Child and Adolescent Psychiatry* 50, no. 7 (2011): 669–80; doi: 10.1016/j.jaac.2011.03.021.

35. C. Kilciksiz, K. Brown, A. Vail, T. Baltrusaitis, L. Pennant, E. Liebson, D. Öngür, L.-P. Morency, and J. Baker, "M111: Quantitative Assessment of Mania and Psychosis during Hospitalization Using Automated Analysis of Face, Voice, and Language," *Schizophrenia Bulletin* 46, Suppl. 1 (2020): S177; doi: 10.1093/schbul/sbaa030.423.

36. Note that some of these signs might indicate a specific diagnosis and may not be representative of the person's overall emotional health. For instance, a person who is oblivious to social cues may suffer from Asperger syndrome, and odd or highly idiosyncratic behaviors may be the result of OCD (obsessive-compulsive disorder).

Chapter 20

1. Stanton E. Samenow, *Inside the Criminal Mind* (New York: Crown Publishers, 2004), 235.

2. Ibid., 239.

3. P. S. Appelbaum, P. C. Robbins, and J. Monahan, "Violence and Delusions: Data from the MacArthur Violence Risk Assessment Study," *American Journal of Psychiatry* 157, no. 4 (2000): 566–72; doi: 10.1176/appi.ajp .157.4.566.

4. Ibid. Statistically, men account for 93 percent of shooting incidents in the workplace.

5. Walter Weintraub, *Verbal Behavior in Everyday Life* (New York: Springer, 1989), 47.

6. Ibid.

7. Statistically, women are more likely to attempt suicide than men, but men are up to three times more likely to succeed in their attempts and die by suicide.

8. Biologically speaking, our vulnerability is partly due to specialized brain cells, called *mirror neurons,* that seek out signals that serve as cues for what is considered proper behavior given the situation. Mirror neurons are responsible for *mass psychogenic illness* (also called *conversation disorder* and previously named *mass hysteria*). A person with this disorder has neurological symptoms—ranging from uncontrolled outbursts to paralysis—that are not related to any known neurological condition and that spread throughout a cohesive group (such as a class in a school or an office) with no root cause other than the subconscious influence of those around them.

9. The term *Werther effect* was coined by Dr. David P. Phillips. He writes, "The increase in the suicide rate was not due to the effect of weekday or monthly fluctuations in motor vehicle fatalities, to holiday weekends, or to yearly linear trends, because the effects were corrected for in the selection and treatment of the control periods, with which the experimental periods are compared." D. P. Phillips, "Suicide, Motor Vehicle Fatalities, and the Mass Media: Evidence toward a Theory of Suggestion," *American Journal of Sociology* 84, no. 5 (1979): 1150–74.

Acknowledgments

It is a great pleasure and privilege to acknowledge the uber-talented professionals at Penguin Random House. First and foremost, a big thank you to my editor at Rodale, Marnie Cochran, whose keen insights and well-honed suggestions have been instrumental in shaping this book.

It really does take a village! To all the talented people in production and design a warm and genuine thank you. Alison Hagge, for her highly diligent and superb copy editing. Anna Bauer for the smart, high-concept cover design. Much appreciation to the designer Andrea Lau, production editor Serena Wang, production manager Jessica Heim, compositor Scribe, whose hard work is evident in every page. To Lindsey Kennedy in publicity and Christina Foxley and Jonathan Sung in marketing, although your efforts have just begun, I am appreciative for all of the time and attention that you've devoted thus far and will no doubt continue to invest.

Thank you to my world-class agent Jim Levine at Greenberg Rostan Literary Agency, for seamlessly ushering this book through the process. And much appreciation to Patricia Weldygo and Patrick Price for their editorial input and insights.

To my colleagues in academia and law enforcement a resounding thank you for your boundless contributions in innumerable ways. You are too many to mention by name and too many who wish to remain nameless. You know who you are, and I am in your debt. The Talmud states that we learn much from our teachers, more from our colleagues, and the most from our students. This timeless wisdom proves itself here, as I especially grateful to my students, including of course, my clients and patients, from whom I have learned the most. I stand in awe of your strength, your courage, and your determination.

I can never fully thank my parents and I remain forever indebted to them. To my extraordinary and loving wife and to my remarkable and precious children, you make it all possible and worthwhile. I am beyond grateful to God for His many blessings and for the opportunity to positively impact on the lives of others.

ABOUT THE AUTHOR

DAVID J. LIEBERMAN, PhD, is an award-winning author and internationally recognized leader in the fields of human behavior and interpersonal relationships. His thirteen books, which have been translated into twenty-eight languages and include two *New York Times* bestsellers, have sold millions of copies worldwide. Dr. Lieberman's works have been featured in hundreds of major publications around the globe, and he appears as a frequent guest expert on national media outlets, such as *The Today Show, The View,* and *Fox & Friends.* He is known for his penetrating insights into human behavior and ability to offer practical psychological tools and strategies to help people lead happier, healthier, and more productive lives. He has trained personnel in every branch of the U.S. military, the FBI, CIA, and NSA, and personally conducts workshops for organizations, governments, and corporations throughout the world—with clients in an astounding 124 countries and thirty-five languages enjoying his online training programs.

Visit DrDavidLieberman.com

From *New York Times* bestselling author
of *Get Anyone to Do Anything*

DAVID LIEBERMAN

The Foolproof Way to Stay Calm and
in Control in Any Conversation or Situation

NEVER

GET

ANGRY

AGAIN

DAVID J. LIEBERMAN, Ph.D.

New York Times Bestselling Author of
Get Anyone to Do Anything and *Never Be Lied to Again*

A comprehensive, holistic look at the underlying
emotional, physical, and spiritual causes of anger,
and what the reader can do to gain perspective
allowing them to never get angry again.